An Altitude SuperGuide

Whistler

& the Sea to Sky Country

An Altitude SuperGuide

Whistler
AND THE
Sea to Sky Country

●

by Constance Brissenden

●

Altitude Publishing Canada Ltd.
Canadian Rockies/Vancouver

Publication Information

Altitude Publishing Canada Ltd.

1500 Railway Avenue, PO Box 1410
Canmore, Alberta T0L 0M0

Copyright 1995 © Altitude
Text Copyright 1995 © Constance Brissenden

Canadian Cataloguing in Publication Data

Brissenden, Connie, 1947-
  Whistler superguide

(SuperGuide)
Includes index.
ISBN 1-55153-029-5

1.Whistler Mountain Region (B.C.)—Guidebooks.
I. Title II. Series.
FC3845. W49B74 1995   917.11'31044
C94-910962-2   F1089.W53B74 1995

Made in Western Canada

Printed and bound in Canada
by Friesens, Altona, Manitoba.

Altitude GreenTree Program

Altitude Publishing will plant in Western Canada twice as many trees as were used in the manufacturing of this product.

Front cover photo:
  Whistler Village
Front cover, inset left:
  Snowboarding
Front cover, inset right:
  Hiking in the Whistler/Blackcomb area
Frontispiece:
  View between Squamish and Whistler
Back cover photo:
  Kids Kamp at Blackcomb

Project Development

Concept/Art Direction	Stephen Hutchings
Design	Stephen Hutchings
Editor	Nancy Flight
Maps	Catherine Burgess
Electronic Page Layout	Sandra Davis, Alison Barr, Nancy Green
Financial Management	Laurie Smith
Index/proofreading	Noeline Bridge

A Note from the Publisher

The world described in Altitude SuperGuides is a unique and fascinating place. It is a world filled with surprise and discovery, beauty and enjoyment, questions and answers. It is a world of people, cities, landscape, animals, and wilderness as seen through the eyes of those who live in, work with, and care for this world. The process of describing this world is also a means of defining ourselves.

It is also a world of relationship, where people derive their meaning from a deep and abiding contact with the land—as well as from each other. And it is this sense of relationship that guides all of us at Altitude to ensure that these places continue to survive and evolve in the decades ahead.

Altitude SuperGuides are books intended to be used as much as read. Like the world they describe, *Altitude SuperGuides* are evolving, adapting, and growing. Please write to us with your comments and observations, and we will do our best to incorporate your ideas into future editions of these books.

Stephen Hutchings
Publisher

Contents

The **Whistler SuperGuide** is organized according to the following colour scheme:

Information and introductory sections.........
Vancouver to Howe Sound ....
Southern Sea to Sky Highway.........................
Introduction to Whistler................................
Northern Sea to Sky Highway.........................
Reference/Index ....

Introduction

Black Tusk

Highway 99—known as the Sea to Sky Highway for its panoramic views of Howe Sound and the Coast Mountains—curves northward from Horseshoe Bay to Whistler Resort and beyond to gold rush country. Only a few hours from the major centres of Vancouver and Victoria, this compact parcel of British Columbia offers countless attractions, including some of the most accessible wilderness escapes in the province.

Many people are drawn to Sea to Sky Country by the lure of Whistler Resort, home of Whistler and Blackcomb mountains. Renowned as North America's premier ski resort, Whistler is also highly recommended as a summer destination. Sociable and sporty, glamorous and rustic, Whistler has many faces, vis-tas, and viewpoints.

"Vancouver to Howe Sound" describes Highway 99, including highlights along the way and how the highway was built. It also discusses the Royal Hudson and gives other information about getting to Whistler. "Southern Sea to Sky Highway" covers the journey along Howe Sound and through the Cheakamus Canyon to Whistler, with side trips into Horseshoe Bay, Britannia Beach, Squamish, Brackendale, and Garibaldi Provincial Park.

Four chapters follow on Whistler Resort (including Whistler and Blackcomb mountains): "Introduction to Whistler," "Whistler in Winter," "Whistler in Summer", and "Whistler for Kids." In these chapters, you'll discover the spectrum of activities offered, from downhill skiing to year-round sports and cultural events.

The final chapter, "Northern Sea to Sky Highway," leads you along the routes beyond

The naming of Whistler

PIONEERS KNEW THE area as London Mountain, a name given to it by Hudson's Bay Company explorers. Local residents later chose to honour the whistler marmot (officially known as the hoary marmot), often seen basking on rocks in the alpine sun. Aptly named, the whistler marmot emits a shrill alarm when confronted with danger. Be forewarned: hang on to your packs in marmot country. These critters will steal away with whatever they can get their paws on.

Whistler, to historic gold rush towns and isolated recreation communities. It includes the Coast Mountain Circle Tour.

Throughout the text, boxes highlight recreational activities, cultural events, contemporary and historical figures, nature, and the history of the area. For your convenience, local amenities are covered throughout the book, with a final reference section at the back.

Selected information about restaurants, accommodation, and shopping has been included. For complete listings of accommodations and camp-

grounds, please see *British Columbia Accommodations*, published annually by the provincial government. Pick it up free of charge at tourist outlets and Infocentres throughout the province. (Infocentres, identifiable by their red, white, and blue signs, offer free maps and up-to-date local information.)

The *Whistler SuperGuide* is designed for every traveller to the area. Whether you are visiting Whistler for a day of skiing, hiking, or browsing, or you are exploring the region on an extended holiday, this guide is your key to its spectacular beauty and impressive recreational services.

Vancouver to Howe Sound

Coast Mountains embraced by clouds

W histler and its surrounding area is undeniably one of the most enjoyable and convenient travel destinations on Canada's West Coast; it is ideal for a day trip or a month-long vacation. Vancouver, British Columbia's largest city and the centre of activity for more than 1.5 million people, is only 20 kilometres from Horseshoe Bay, where our tour begins. Victoria, the provincial capital, is almost as handy. From Vancouver Island, visitors heading for Vancouver and, ultimately, Whistler, depart from either Swartz Bay, 32 kilometres north of Victoria, or Nanaimo's Departure Bay. From Victoria, you'll arrive in Tsawwassen on Highway 99, a short 30 kilometres from Vancouver. Leaving Departure Bay in Nanaimo, the ferry docks conveniently in Horseshoe Bay.

A half-hour's scenic drive from Vancouver, Horseshoe Bay is reached by crossing the Lions Gate Bridge or Second Narrows Bridge (both offer the first of many spectacular views) as access points for the North Shore's Upper Levels Highway; follow the signs for Trans-Canada Highway 1/Highway 99. Below the bridges is Burrard Inlet, dotted with international vessels basking peacefully before unloading or loading. The hamlet of Horseshoe Bay is a convenient place to stop for refreshments or to gas up on your way up the 100-kilometre-long section of Highway 99 to Whistler. The next gas station is in Squamish, 40 kilometres north.

Enroute on Highway 99

Referred to locally as the Squamish Highway, and dubbed the Sea to Sky Highway by the tourism wordsmiths of the province, Highway 99 has undergone significant improvements in the past few years.

Originally a logging and homesteading road hacked

out of the coastal rain forest, the highway snakes northward, hugging the granite cliffs overlooking Howe Sound. The views make it difficult to keep your eyes on the road—take advantage of frequent pullovers rather than risk an accident. As you'll soon discover, Highway 99 demands alertness. Tight curves, speeding drivers, unexpected changes in weather, and the occasional rock fall add challenge to driving conditions. It's best to travel during the day, if possible.

At Squamish, a growth centre of over 12,000 residents, you'll find all amenities along or just off the highway. After Squamish, Highway 99 heads inland, continuing on through the narrow Cheakamus Canyon to Whistler Resort. After Brackendale, the highway parallels the Cheakamus River, which is clearly visible on the left until it meets the Cheakamus Dam and Daisy Lake, an artificial reservoir used to generate hydroelectric power. The original Daisy Lake was one-twentieth its current size.

Explore Whistler Resort and then some

It's no surprise that Whistler Resort is consistently awarded international kudos for its skiing facilities and services. As you enter the resort, ski getaways rise on rocky precipices overlooking the highway—a taste of luxuries to come. Luckily for most visitors, there are more affordable accommodations available. You needn't spend your life's earnings to enjoy what the resort has to offer, since accommo-

dations to suit every pocketbook, from budget to deluxe, are available.

Two mountains double the fun of Whistler Resort. The first to be established as a ski destination was Whistler Mountain in 1965. Blackcomb Mountain, the newcomer on the scene, has been in business since 1980. At 2440 metres, Blackcomb is the higher. Whistler comes in at just under at 2178 metres.

The heart of the resort is Whistler Village, with Whistler Creek and the bench lands of Blackcomb Mountain also offering amenities. The signs of success are everywhere. In 1993 alone, $90 million worth of new projects were in some stage of construction. Exceptional press, including being named North America's top ski resort, hasn't hurt either. The 1993-94 winter season was Whistler Mountain's busiest ever, with a record 665,000 skiers enjoying the slopes.

Happily for many visitors, Whistler and area is geared for more than downhill skiing. A substantial number of tourism-related companies have followed the mountains' leads and now offer a host of recreation packages, including heli-hiking, snowmobiling, dog sled tours, canoeing, river-rafting, horseback riding, and mountain biking to serve visitors year-round. As a result, summer is catching up with winter in popularity.

Moving on

Beyond this world-class ski resort, Highway 99 continues its Coast Mountain Circle Tour through Pemberton and

Mount Currie and eastward to Lillooet. Endless outdoor activities provide access to a wilder British Columbia: four-wheel-drive back roads, washboard summer highways crossing remote mountain ranges, natural hot springs, and tumbledown ghost towns. Ideal for camping buffs, the area is also comfortable and easy to tour for those who prefer accommodations with hot and cold running water.

Before 1992, visitors beyond Mount Currie contended with the unpaved Duffey Lake Road route to Lillooet. Today the road is a paved extension of Highway 99, making the Coast Mountain Circle Tour increasingly popular. The exception is a 9-kilometre section passing through the Mount Currie Reserve. Disagreements with the provincial government about land use seem to ensure that this unique segment of the highway will remain a gravel road for some time.

How far is it?	
Route ....Distance (km)	
Horseshoe Bay to:	
Vancouver	20
Lions Bay	11
Britannia Beach	32
Squamish	44
Brackendale	54
Whistler Resort	100
Pemberton	135
Mount Currie	141
Birken	164
D'Arcy	179
Lillooet	235
Gold Bridge (via Hurley Road)	217
Gold Bridge (via Lillooet)	344
Bralorne (via Lillooet)	351

The islands of Howe Sound bask in the sunlight

Continuing northwest beyond Lillooet along Carpenter Lake Road, you'll find yourself in Gold Rush Country. Here, in the midst of the Cariboo-Chilcotin region's long, sweeping hills and mountain wilderness, you'll find backcountry hospitality, including guided tours by plane and on horseback.

If travelling elsewhere in the province, you'll want to consult the *British Columbia Interior SuperGuide* and *Vancouver CityGuide*. Both provide extensive information for visitors exploring adjacent regions, including additional information about the Coast Mountain Circle Tour. After leaving Highway 99 and Sea to Sky Country, you may choose to join Trans-Canada Highway 1 at Cache Creek, where you can return to Vancouver

or head east to Kamloops to explore British Columbia's vast Interior region.

Hewn from rock and stone

Pavement comes slowly to some parts of British Columbia. In 1958, a 1000-car cavalcade led by the premier of the province celebrated the completion of a paved highway to Squamish. It wasn't until the mid-1960s that the tarmac was extended all the way to Whistler, then known as Alta Lake. And it was only in 1992 that the link between Pemberton and Lillooet (the former Duffey Lake Road) moved beyond gravel dust bowl with a $22.5 million upgrade to pavement.

The terrain along Highway 99 was, and is to this day, a road builder's nightmare,

constantly testing engineering capabilities. Repeated freezing and thawing during winter months expands the joints between the rocks that line the highway. Because the joints in certain sections are at a 50-degree angle and parallel to the road, friction can't stop loosened boulders from falling.

Cliffs draped in steel mesh, evidence of intensive and continuous work to prevent slides, help contain rocks and boulders. In other areas, the highway is built on concrete blocks to put space between the road and falling rocks. A kilometre beyond Montizambert Creek, a cliff prone to rock falls has been sprayed with concrete to contain loose materials.

Cutting a road into the side of a mountain and trying to minimize rock fall hazards is only half the story. Before extensive roadwork was done, nature often unleashed such a fury that bridges, property, and lives were lost. On Charles Creek and Newman Creek, as well as others along the highway, massive concrete debris catch basins now protect travellers from the destructive force that turns small mountain creeks into torrents of rocks, trees, and water.

The most visible concrete catch basin, similar to a dam, is located on Charles Creek. In 1983, before the structure was built, a debris flow tossed a 99-tonne railway bridge deck into Howe Sound as if it were a toy.

Longtime locals have their own names for sections of Highway 99, monikers like Slide Hill and Suicide Hill. Today, thanks to continuous improvements, such as a recent $500,000 safety upgrade, hazards for visitors have been reduced. Still, caution is advised at all times. Since improvements are constantly being made, you may experience short delays while highway crews continue their work.

A crew strengthens the granite rock face overlooking Highway 99

The Railway from Nowhere to Nowhere

It was known as the Railway from Nowhere to Nowhere, and its initials, PGE (for Pacific Great Eastern), mocked as Please Go Easy, Prince George Eventually, and Past God's Endurance.

Founded by industrialists on February 27, 1912, the Pacific Great Eastern Railway was ill-fated from the start. After raising the princely sum of $5 million to build a rail line to BC's northern areas, the great 19th-century railway boom went bust. By 1918, PGE's investors were left with a popular but money-losing passenger service between North and West Vancouver and an unfinished line between Squamish and Quesnel.

The mainline of the Pacific Great Eastern was constructed northward from Squamish, then known as Newport. For many years, the connection between Vancouver and the start of the steel was by Union Steamships. After the train was loaded at the Squamish Dock, it moved up the line to the town of Squamish, picking up more passengers and mail before heading northward.

In 1918, the provincial government took over completion of the line from Chasm, at mile 174 (kilometre 280) from Squamish. By 1921, it had only reached Quesnel, another 273 kilometres northward. Cottonwood Canyon, north of Quesnel, was the main obstacle. Finally, in 1952, steel was eventually laid through to Prince George.

The Pacific Great Eastern reflected the more relaxed lifestyle of an earlier time. Frequent stops were the order of the day, to pick up or deliver passengers, lumber, goods, and even cattle. Train crews carried many precious items,

EVEN TODAY, with frequent passing lanes along the route, it's not difficult to imagine a time when passing another car on Highway 99 was reserved for the foolish or reckless. There's still room for caution: heed the following guidelines for a safe journey.

Speed zones are posted in kilometres per hour. Some standard zones are 50 km/h (30 mph), 80 km/h (50 mph), and 90 km/h (55 mph).

Tailgaters can be a problem. Slow down and make room between your vehicle and the one in front so that others may pass. Use passing lanes as instructed. Or, when safe to do so, pull over to let faster vehicles pass. Pull off the road to check your map.

Seat belts and child restraints are mandatory for all occupants. Motorcyclists must wear approved safety helmets.

Keep headlights on at all times. The use of headlights increases visibility and reduces the chance of an accident by as much as 20 percent.

Driving with more than .08 percent blood alcohol content is illegal. Don't drink and drive.

Stay alert! Wildlife, road repair crews, speeding drivers, slippery gravel, flying rocks, rock falls, dust, washouts, ice, rain, snow, avalanches, and vehicle accidents can cause sudden problems. Your tires, brakes, wipers, and cooling system should be in top condition before you travel.

Adjust your speed to road conditions. Slow down to stay alive.

Drive the Sea to Sky Highway with lights on

from tobacco to the Vancouver newspaper, northward to isolated homesteads.

In 1956, the railway took delivery of six self-propelled rail diesel cars (RDCs) from the Budd Corporation of Philadelphia. The fleet of RDCs—the mainstay of BC Rail's scheduled northbound service—now comprises 12 units. Today's BC Rail Dayliner passenger service runs to Prince George, 740 kilometres from the start of its journey at the North Vancouver Station.

Travelling northbound are foodstuffs, liquor, beer, construction materials, and chemicals. Southbound cargo includes forest products, beer, and scrap metal.

BC Rail

The BC Rail Dayliner departs daily from its North Vancouver and Whistler stations; the trip is approximately 2.5 hours each way. From Whistler, the Dayliner continues north to Prince George, a distance of 744 kilometres (462 miles). You'll pass through Pemberton, Mount Currie, Birken, D'Arcy, and Anderson Lake enroute to Lilloeet. South Shalalth is the site of BC Hy- do's Bridge River Power House. Adult, senior, and children's rates are available. Tickets and information are available at the North Vancouver Station or on board from the conductor. BC Transit provides shuttle bus service to

Other ways to travel

Early Brackendale stage

1. BUS
Some buses require reservations.
- Blackcomb Mountain Ski Bus: 662-8051
- Charter Bus Lines of British Columbia: 270-4442
- Glacier Coach Lines: 932-2705
- Gray Line of Vancouver: 682-2877
- International Stage Lines: 279-6135
- Maverick Coach Lines: 255-1171
- Perimeter Transportation Airport Express: 261-2299
- Top Hat Mini Coach: 681-3444
- Whistler Mountain Ski Express: 244-3744

2. CAR
Car rental in Whistler:
- Avis Rent A Car: 938-1331
- Budget Rent A Car: 932-1236
- Hertz Rent A Car: 938-0020
- Thrifty Car Rental: 938-0302

Car rental in Squamish:
- Hertz Rent A Car: 892-2044
- U-Drive: 892-3588

In Vancouver: Check the Yellow Pages under "Automobile Renting & Leasing"

3. TAXIS AND LIMOUSINES
- Blackcomb Taxi and Limousine: 932-3399
- Mountain Limousine: 932-5220
- Sea to Sky Taxi: 932-3333
- Town & Country Chauffeurs: 932-6468
- Whistler Taxi and Limousine: 938-3333

4. AIR
- Blackcomb Helicopters: 938-1700
- Canadian Helicopters: 278-5502
- Corporate Helicopters: 932-3512
- Glacier Air Tours: 898-9016

- Helijet Airways: 938-1878
- Pemberton Helicopters: 894-6919
- Prime Air: 685-7722 (Seattle Airport-Pemberton Airport)
- Vancouver Helicopters: 938-3345
- Whistler Air Service: 932-6615

5. ACCOMMODATION AND TOUR PACKAGES
- The Whistler Experience: 683-2772. One-day excursions from Vancouver.
- Canada-West Accommodations: 987-9338/932-2667. Dual-mountain ski packages with accommodations.
- Peak Adventure Network, Whistler: 932-2126.
- Whistler Central Reservations: 664-5625/932-4222/1-800-944-7853 in Canada and US. Accommodation packages with skiing or golf.

Salvaged from the wrecking yard, the Royal Hudson is the pride of BC Rail

the North Vancouver Station from downtown Vancouver and from the North Vancouver SeaBus Terminal. Call 261-5100 for details. The Whistler station is located on Lake Placid Road (Whistler Creek) with free connecting bus service to Whistler Village. Call 984-5246/631-3500.

The Royal Hudson

BC Rail's famed Royal Hudson steam train runs to Squamish Wednesdays through Sundays, as well as on holiday Mondays, from June to mid-September. If you like, take the train one way and the *MV/Britannia* passenger ferry the other way for a 6.5-hour return trip.

For information, call BC Rail (984-5246/631-3500) or Harbour Ferries Ltd./1st Tours (688-7246/1-800-663-1500).

You may also write: BC Rail Ltd. Passenger Services, P.O. Box 8770, Vancouver, BC V6B 4X6. Telephone: 932-4003 (Whistler); 631-3501 (Vancouver).

From the Squamish train station, you can also continue on to Whistler by motorcoach. Day return and overnight packages are available from Alpine Adventure Tours (683-0209).

Steaming up Howe Sound

Superlatives are the order of the day when it comes to BC Rail's Royal Hudson, the last steam locomotive still in service in Canada. Steaming up Howe Sound, its throaty whistle has been described as "the sound of summer."

Passing over trestles and through six tunnels, this is a magnificent journey on a train that was destined, more than once, for the scrap heap. Like a cat, this train appears to have nine lives.

Since 1974, the Royal Hudson has travelled the

64-kilometre North Vancouver-Squamish line more than 2000 times. Passengers do not have to be steam enthusiasts to appreciate the majesty of this proud engine, one of the province's most popular tourist attractions.

The Royal Hudson began its journey in 1940, built for fast passenger service by Montreal Locomotive Works for the Canadian Pacific Railway (CPR). The name Hudson was given to locomotives with a 4-6-4 wheel arrangement; "Royal" was added after CPR

Hudson 2850 carried King George VI from Quebec City to Vancouver in 1938. Another honour bestowed on all Hudson class engines after the King's visit was a crown on the forward part of the running board.

Early in its career, the Royal Hudson pulled transcontinental passenger trains between Revelstoke and Vancouver. A serious derailment in 1956 along Vancouver's Burrard Inlet, however, led many to believe that the locomotive was beyond repair. A

timely reprieve resulted in refurbishment of the train. When the renovations were complete, the Royal Hudson was transferred to Winnipeg for further duty.

After only two more years of service, dieselization and the obsolescence of steam finally caught up with the Royal Hudson. Ignominiously, the once-proud engine was designated as scrap. After years of rusting in the scrap line, it was granted a stay of execution from the cutter's torch and sent back to Vancouver in 1964 to be part of a proposed railway museum.

Again, fate intervened. The museum never opened and the Royal Hudson faced an uncertain future. It sat in a Vancouver roundhouse until it was finally acquired by the Province of British Columbia in 1973, to be lovingly restored to operating perfection.

The inaugural run of the service from North Vancouver to Squamish was made on June 20, 1974. In 1982, the BC government formed the Royal Hudson Steam Train Society to oversee operation of the train, and BC Rail contracted the use of it. In 1990, BC Rail took over the society.

Today, the 2860 Royal Hudson and vintage 3716 engines chugging along Howe Sound are the only steam locomotives in scheduled mainline service on a North American railway.

Fortunately, the Royal Hudson survived. Wearing the Coat of Arms of the Province of British Columbia, this majestic locomotive serves as a legacy to the age of steam travel.

Popular at home and abroad

A tour group of Japanese cyclists, students from a women's physical education college, on the Pemberton Portage Road to D'Arcy

AS THESE 1993 SUMMER STATISTICS and 1992-93 winter statistics show, Whistler Resort attracts visitors both from home and abroad. Point of origin (ranked by number):

Summer	Winter
1. Canada	1. Canada
2. United States	2. United States
3. United Kingdom	3. Japan
4. Japan	4. United Kingdom
5. France	5. Australia
6. Germany	6. Germany
7. Australia	7. New Zealand
8. New Zealand	8. France

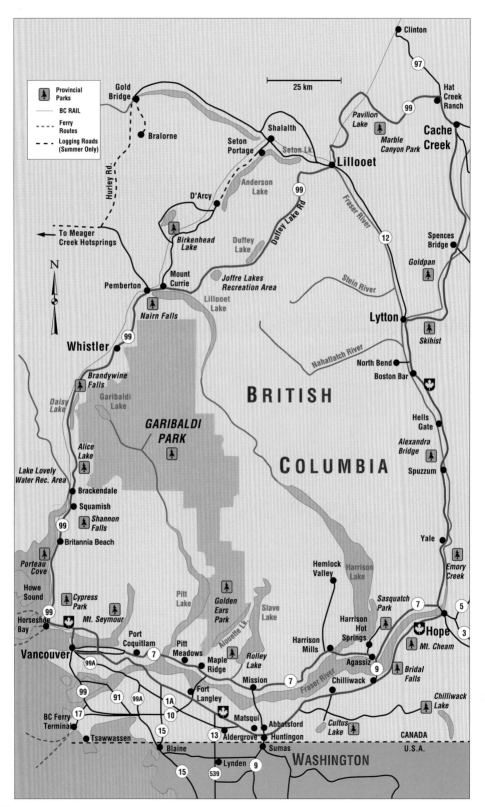

Southern Sea to Sky Highway

Howe Sound lies nestled in a sea of peaks

It is easy to see why Sea to Sky Highway is an apt name for Highway 99. On a sunny summer day, the West Coast rain forest is almost tropical in its lushness; in the rain and fog, ocean and mountains fuse with the subtlety of a Chinese landscape painting. Heading north, Howe Sound stretches lazily on your left. More than 40 kilometres long, it is a fiord, the product of glaciation more than 10,000 years ago. The cliffs to your right belong to the Coast Mountain Range, which extends eastward to the interior plateaus and runs northward along the edge of the continent for 1700 kilometres to the Yukon. These mountains are mostly granite, having cooled underground over 100 million years ago and eventually been uplifted; their creation leaves a legacy of rugged beauty and challenging isolation.

The original inhabitants were the Coast Salish people to the south and the Interior Salish beyond present-day Whistler. British Columbia was one of the last North American frontiers to be explored by Europeans. With the Fraser gold rush of the late 1850s and 1860s, the land began to be transformed. By 1873, a rough and dangerous horse trail was hand-cut from Howe Sound to the farming community of Pemberton. Over the next five years, with the help of the BC government, it was improved somewhat to become the Howe Sound-Lillooet Cattle Trail.

Today an estimated 20,000 people live in Sea to Sky Country from Horseshoe Bay, a community of just over 1000 residents located in West Vancouver, to Whistler Resort, which has a permanent population of 5000. Beyond Whistler, the regional district's population is only 5500, the majority of whom live in Lillooet.

Driving tips on backcountry roads

WHEN HEADING FOR the backcountry: check with the nearest BC Forest Service office, especially if you are exploring a backroad for the first time.

Rules of the road give logging trucks the right-of-way

- When driving on logging roads, backroads, and even paved highways, be aware of one very basic rule: logging trucks rule supreme. All trucks and industrial vehicles have the right-of-way on logging roads. Large, powerful, and with limited manoeuvrability, logging trucks fly along both unpaved backcountry roads and paved highways with equal speed. Motorists must hustle to the side when these vehicles appear.
- If you encounter a logging truck, particularly on logging roads, use extreme caution and obey all posted signs. Using logging roads without due caution and preparation is an invitation to tragedy.
- Always use your seat belts.
- Logging trucks use all or most of the road. When you see a logging truck—or any other heavy-equipment vehicle—get to a turnout and let it go by. A turnout may be on either side of the road: whichever side it's on, it's your responsibility to get to it.
- Logging trucks move quickly, and backcountry roads often have sharp, blind corners. For your own safety, stay alert and ready to take evasive action.
- The speed limit on backcountry roads, unless otherwise posted, is 80 kilometres per hour, often too fast for a light truck or car. Use caution; stay in compete control of your vehicle.
- Obey all road signs. If a sign says a road is closed, that's what it means. If you proceed, you do so at great risk.

- Don't block a road or stop in the road. If you stop, park well off to the side.
- Drive with your lights on.
- Don't haul a travel trailer on a backcountry road. Loaded logging rigs can't back up steep grades. Having to make way by backing your car and trailer down a steep mountain road could be fatal.
- Logging trucks use radios to communicate. Road signs indicate the radio frequency in use. If you have a suitable two-way radio, announce your location—check the kilometre markers along the road—and direction of travel. Drive with the same degree of caution, whether you use your radio or not.
- Don't trust your CB. It does not use the same frequency as a logging truck radio.
- Watch for sweepers, extra-long logs (up to 21 metres) hauled by logging rigs. On a steep logging road with tight curves, they could literally sweep your car off the edge.
- Stop if you find an immobile logging truck. When it's clear to go or when the driver waves you on,

proceed with caution.
- Watch for hazardous road damage such as washouts, slides, and blown-down trees.
- Be prepared. Be sure to take the following: emergency food, fire extinguisher, extra fuel, first-aid kit, warm clothing, waterproof matches, sleeping bags, tool kit. If you get lost, stay with your vehicle. If you check in at the BC Forest Service office before your trip, help is likely to come if you need it.
- Over the years, the BC Forest Service's road network has grown to more than 32,000 kilometres throughout British Columbia. Before travelling the backroads, check with a local BC Forest Service (BCFS) district office. Maps of logging roads and recreation facilities are provided, as well as up-to-date reports on road conditions.

For more information, contact the Squamish Forest District, 42000 Loggers Lane, Squamish, BC V0N 3G0, telephone 898-2100. North of Whistler, call the Pemberton Field Office (April-October) at 894-6112.

Proud Nations

The girls, best friends from the Anderson Lake Band, couldn't be more than 11 years old. Dressed in their dance regalia, bright dresses trimmed with ribbon, they're too young to know how important they are to the future and the cultural resurgence taking place in Native communities across British Columbia. Together with a dozen or so other children from the small community of Anderson Lake, the girls are learning traditional dancing, drumming, and singing. At the band's summer powwow, held in August, they were there, front and centre, dancing enthusiastically.

Guests at local powwows, both Native and non-Native, are welcome at these annual gatherings. Some are traditional, with everything except handicrafts offered as a gift from the community to the participants. Other powwows charge an entry fee, with arts

A dancer in full Plains regalia performs a traditional grass dance

and crafts, bannock (a deep fried bread), and hoshan (a beverage made from soapberries) for sale. Unlike the traditional powwows, these powwows offer hefty prizes to winners of dance competitions.

Through these and other gatherings, Native people are celebrating their survival with renewed pride. At the time of the West Coast's first European contact in the 1770s, 40 percent of Canada's Native population lived in British Columbia, for the most part along the coastline and main western rivers. Estimates place their numbers between 80,000 and 125,000 people. Over two dozen languages were spoken, and active trading took place along the Pacific Coast and into the Interior.

For centuries, Coast Salish lived along Burrard Inlet, Howe Sound, and the Squamish and Cheakamus rivers. Five main reserves exist

Native art today

TRADITIONAL SOCIETIES were notable for their artistic symbolism, evident in the images carved or painted on objects used in daily life. Today art continues to be a force in Native life. Masks, prints, carvings, jewellery, and totem poles are highly prized. A mask carved by a major artist, for example, can sell for as much as $15,000. In addition to creating museum-quality pieces, many Native people make their livelihood as artisans. Their work can be purchased in galleries and gift shops, as well as directly from local artists.

The potlatch ceremony

POTLATCHES WERE HELD by the aboriginal people of the West Coast to celebrate weddings, funerals, and name giving. A Coast Salish host would invite people from across his tribe's territory, which includes Vancouver Island and parts of the United States, then give everyone gifts to show his respect. It was a great honour to be invited to a potlatch. Many days and nights of dancing, singing, eating, and gift giving marked the ceremony.

White settlers knew when a potlatch was in the making. Masked aboriginal people would walk up and down the streets of Squamish, a drummer announcing their way. Settlers considered it an honour to be invited.

The Federal Department of Indian Affairs outlawed the potlatch ceremony in 1884. They are now slowly returning to the West Coast.

today, the Sta-mish (South Squamish), Kowtain (North Yards), see-aye-chum (Eagle Run/Brackendale), Wai-wa-kum (Brackendale), and the chee-Yamush (Cheekye/Cheakamus). The chee-Ya-mush is the largest reserve in the Squamish area.

Known for being peace-able, Squamish people got on well with other Salish tribes, such as the Musqueam, Nanaimo, Saanich, Cowichan, Sechelt, Lummi, and Sto:Lo. Their principal enemies were the Kwagiulth from the central coast and Tsilhqot'in from the Interior.

Interior Salish included those of the Lower Lillooet liv-ing in the Pemberton area and several villages above Lillooet Lake (now known as the Mount Currie Band). Upper Lillooet people inhabited vil-lages on Anderson and Seton lakes and are now known as the Anderson Lake Band and the Seton Lake Band. Inventive and capable people, the Salish developed many technologies, among them cedar bark basketry, wool weaving (using material from woolly dogs, mountain sheep, and moun-

Horseshoe Bay retains its historic charm

tain goats), oceangoing ca-noes, and underground houses.

The aboriginal people of British Columbia experienced the same fate as other North American Native people. On the West Coast, Indian wars were not needed to suppress their numbers—epidemics,

dislocation, starvation, alcohol, and violence tragically did the job. Some groups were so re-duced in numbers that they were compelled to join other groups for survival.

By 1835, after a series of devastating smallpox epi-demics, BC's Native popula-tion had dropped to

Horseshoe Bay amenities

HORSESHOE BAY is located in the District of West Vancouver, extending north on Highway 99 to Sunset Beach Park. Ameni-ties include BC Ferries, restau-rants and takeout service, a motel, a bank machine, a postal outlet, gift shops, art galleries, a grocery store, a marina, a pay telephone, and a gas station. Fill up in Horseshoe Bay. The next gas station is in Squamish, 44 kilometres north.

Horseshoe Bay contact numbers

TOURIST INFORMATION:
West Vancouver Chamber of Commerce: 926-6614
• Emergency (Fire, Police, Ambulance): 911
• Police non-emergency: 922-4141
• Lions Gate Hospital, 231 E. 15th Street, North Van-couver: 988-3131 Hospital Emergency: 984-5799 (serves Horseshoe Bay to Village of Lions Bay)

• BC Ferries: 277-0277
• BC Rail: 986-2012
• Department of Highways: 660-8800
• Roads: contact the Trouble Line: 926-2581
• Sewell's Marina: 921-3474
• Cormorant Marine Water Taxi: 947-2243
• The Horseshoe Bay Motel: 921-7454

approximately 70,000. In the 1880s, smallpox spread to the Squamish Valley. Many died, and five major villages had to be burned with others along the coast. The lowest ebb was in 1929, when the census recorded only 22,600 aboriginal people in BC. Since 1939, however, the growth rate has increased. Ninety thousand people of aboriginal descent now live in

Horseshoe Bay has always been a scenic destination

Pioneers of Horseshoe Bay

TOM SEWELL'S father, Dan, was born in London, England, and came to Canada in 1903. Heading for Edmonton, he successfully ran his own construction company. World War I took Dan overseas with the 63rd Battalion in 1914. On his return in 1918, business did not flourish. Through a friend, he heard of remote Horseshoe Bay and the fabulous fishing it had to offer. Jumping a rail car to Vancouver, Dan went to have a look. It was love at first sight. By 1922, he'd moved his wife, Eva, and their two sons, Art and Tom, out to the West Coast, taking whatever construction jobs he and his sons could find in Vancouver.

Sewell kept his dream of Horseshoe Bay alive. A waterfront property for sale caught his eye, the only one with a private beach. Owned by a Mr. Thorpe, it was the original summer home of the

Tom Sewell

wealthy Roedde family of Vancouver. Thorpe agreed to sell; by 1931, the Sewell family was installed in its new home.

Whytecliff Lodge, which stood at the present-day location of Troll's Restaurant, was also part of the deal. It was moved from its Bay Street location to Sewell's waterfront property, where the Boathouse Restaurant now stands.

Dan Sewell's lodge and marina eventually became fishing headquarters for many avid fishers, including theatrical, political, and sports figures from the 1930s

onward. Crooner Bing Crosby and cowboy Roy Rogers were among the repeat visitors. News of the excellent fishing spread across North America through the thriving vaudeville theatre in Vancouver. Top-billed entertainers played Vancouver by night and then motored to Horseshoe Bay to fish during the day.

The Lodge, converted into a general store after the top floor was gutted by a 1955 fire, was finally replaced in 1980. It is open today as the Boathouse, a specialty seafood restaurant. Sewell's Marina, run by Dan Sewell's grandson and namesake, continues to provide boat rentals, charters, and marine services.

Tom Sewell, now in his eighties, still resides in the Roedde house with his wife, Laverne. The house is located just off the pay parking lot.

British Columbia on and off reserves.

Horseshoe Bay

Horseshoe Bay was known to its Native inhabitants as Chai-hai, meaning a low, sizzling noise, probably made by small fish jumping along the shore in the evening. Today a more likely sound is the hoot of a BC Ferry enroute to Vancouver Island,

A totem pole in Horseshoe Bay Park honours First Nations' achievements

the Sunshine Coast, or Bowen Island. The terminal located in the bay is one of British Columbia's busiest, providing a link to outlying destinations.

In spite of progress, Horseshoe Bay still retains much of its original charm. With a population of just over 1000 people tucked into the nooks and crannies in the surrounding hills, this once little-known summer hideaway maintains a community feeling.

A small but inviting park curves along the bay, providing a convenient view of comings and goings on the water and a playground for active children.

Steps away are restaurants, coffeehouses, ice cream shops, gift stores, galleries, and a marina. Troll's Restaurant, with its famous fish and chips takeout counter, is across from the park.

Two totem poles commemorate the contributions of BC's Native commu-

nities. One, near Troll's Restaurant, was carved by Coast Tsimshian Chief William Jeffrey and his son Rupert in 1975. A second pole, a Kwagiulth bear pole, was carved by Tony Hunt of the Kwawkewlth Band of northern Vancouver Island, in 1966.

People have been coming to Horseshoe Bay for day trips and holidays since the early 1900s. One of the first families, the Roeddes, built their summer home by shipping it in sections by water from Vancouver.

Commanding the only private beach, the Roeddes installed cultivated lawns, which rolled down to the water's edge and were fenced for privacy. No stores existed and all supplies were packed along. If food ran low, it was an adventure to row across Howe Sound to Bowen Island to buy homemade bread from its bakery. Every year, Mr. Roedde would bring the 70 employees from his Vancouver

printing shop out via the railway for their annual picnic.

In 1922, Dan Sewell, the first of Horseshoe Bay's four generations of Sewells, moved to the bay. The Sewells become a legend on the West Coast for their knack for fishing and boat building.

Another influential family moved into Horseshoe Bay in 1946. Troll's Restaurant, founded by Joe and Dorothy Troll, is still operated by the family, with a third generation now on board. From the windows of Troll's dining room, you can watch the ferries ply the waters of Howe Sound while you indulge in BC's famous fresh fish.

Ferries

FERRIES AND WATER TAXIS have plied the waters of Horseshoe Bay to Bowen Island, Anvil Island, and Squamish since the early days. Locals fondly remember the Sannies, running to Bowen Island loaded with excited children on Sunday outings.

BC Ferries depart from Horseshoe Bay on a regular, daily basis. How long does it take to get where you're going?

Snug Cove (Bowen Island): 20 minutes via the *Queen of Capilano*

Langdale (Sunshine Coast):

35 minutes via the *Queen of Cowichan*

Departure Bay (Nanaimo): 95 minutes via the *Queen of Oak Bay* or the *Queen of Surrey*

For more information, call the BC Ferries 24-hour information line: 277-0277. For reservations call 669-1211 (Vancouver), or write BC Ferries, 1112 Fort Street, Victoria, BC V8V 4V2.

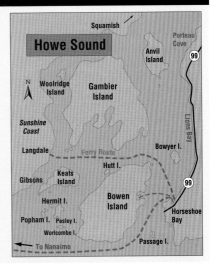

Island lore

AS YOU TRAVEL the Sea to Sky Highway, islands dot Howe Sound to your left. Among them are Bowen, a Vancouver bedroom community with a full-time population of 2500 to 3000 (3500 to 4000 in summer), Bowyer (a private island owned by local families), Gambier (recreation-oriented; accessible by BC Ferries, private boat, or water taxi), and the rugged, largely uninhabited Anvil Island.

Located at the entrance to Howe Sound, Bowen is the largest island visible, 12.5 kilometres long and 6.5 kilometres across at its widest point. Its harbour, Snug Cove, is a small but welcoming village, complete with pub and shops and a handy trail just minutes from the dock. For an inexpensive excursion, leave your car behind.

Bowen Island's history is intriguing:

Native people originally used the island as a summer camping ground.

In 1791, Spaniards of the sloop *Santa Saturnia,* led by Narvaez, were the first Europeans to visit.

Captain George Vancouver made no mention of Bowen Island in his logs. The island was named by Captain George Henry Richards after Rear Admiral James Bowen, who fought in the Napoleonic Wars.

The first settlers arrived in the 1870s. They soon poisoned all the wolves that once roamed the island.

In 1887, the Croft and Angus lumber company bought lot 492, a parcel of 344 hectares of forest. In 1889, it was sold to the Victoria Lumber and Manufacturing Company, one of the largest lumber companies in the United States.

Because of a depression, little logging took place until 1896, but by 1899, business was booming. Orders were turned down until the mill could be expanded.

In the 1890s, prize fights—illegal in Vancouver—were held here.

In 1901, white union fishermen kidnapped non-union Japanese fishermen and marooned them on the island.

A 1902 government report stated, "The fish can be literally raked out of the water in Howe Sound."

By 1909, the entire 344 hectares of lot 492 were logged out. Shortly after, Montreal-based Western Explosives Inc. bought the land for a dynamite plant. Many of its 80 workers were Chinese or Japanese. A series of explosions killed 11 untrained workers.

In the 1920s, Bowen Island's bays were used by rumrunners— hence the name Smugglers Cove.

Since the 1980s, pollution from the pulp mills on Howe Sound occasionally results in closures for bottom fish and crabs.

In 1994, house prices on Bowen Island ranged from $200,000 to more than $1 million.

Enroute to Britannia Beach

The community of Lions Bay (population 1330) began with humble cottages near the shoreline. With the opening of Highway 99, expensive new homes were built higher uphill.

Because many of the residences are constructed on an outwash fan, homeowners are all too familiar with the power of nature. In February 1983, a debris torrent of soil, boulders, and trees raged down Alberta Creek, devastating all in its path. Thirty minutes later, all road bridges and five homes were destroyed.

Massive engineering projects now protect Lions Bay from future flows. Looking up Harvey Creek, note the concrete spillway extending from the catch basin, a gigantic structure dug into the ground to catch debris, the most destructive component of any

Lions Bay amenities

LIONS BAY information is available from the Lions Bay Municipal Hall (921-9333 or 921-9811). The Lions Bay General Store, offering groceries, postal service, specialty coffees and takeout pizza, is open seven days a week (921-6344). To launch your boat, call the Lions Bay Marina (921-7510). The marina sells gas and oil for boats, and has a public washroom. To get to the marina, turn right at the Lions Bay exit, then left, and watch for the sign.

Diving at Porteau Cove

FRONTING HOWE SOUND, the most southerly fiord in North America, Porteau Cove Provincial Park was established in 1981. Just minutes from shore, divers have a veritable underwater playground. Above water, there are warm and cold diver's showers open year-round, 24 hours a day.

At Porteau, much of the water is relatively shallow, averaging 30 metres, courtesy of a gigantic pile of rubble (or moraine) that stretches across Howe Sound, almost dividing the fiord into two distinct basins. It was deposited by the glacier that helped create the sound.

Helping nature along is an artificial reef and collection of sunken shipwrecks, installed with the cooperation of various BC diving associations. Coloured markers floating in the water show the locations of wrecks, ships, and barges intentionally sunk for use by recreational divers. In the Jungle Gym area, an artificial reef has been created from concrete bridge sections, blocks, and pipes. Wrecks include the *Nakaya,* a former minesweeper; the

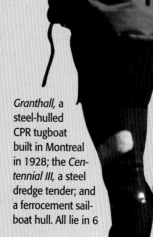

Granthall, a steel-hulled CPR tugboat built in Montreal in 1928; the *Centennial III,* a steel dredge tender; and a ferrocement sailboat hull. All lie in 6 to 18 metres of water and are easily explored by people of all skill levels.

Over 100 marine animal species, including lingcod, plumrose anemones, sponges, octopus, wolf eel, and several types of shrimp flourish in this important habitat. Howe Sound also supports populations of chum, coho, pink, and chinook salmon.

For more information on diving in Porteau Cove, contact BC Parks Visitor Services at 898-3678. Recommended reading: *141 Dives in the Protected Waters of Washington and British Columbia* by Betty Pratt-Johnson (Gordon Soules Book Publishers, 1352B Marine Drive, West Vancouver, BC V7T 1B5).

torrent. After a torrent, debris is scooped out of the basin by bulldozers.

Lions Bay is located behind the Lions, the Lower Mainland's famous twin peaks. The two thumblike peaks, known as the Two Sisters in Native mythology, reign over Vancouver. From Lions Bay, a popular but challenging trail leads to these landmarks. The hike up the 1220-metre elevation gain takes six hours. It's best attempted from late June to October, preferably with a knowledgeable guide.

Continuing north of Lions Bay, the highway descends alongside a gravel quarry. Other sand and gravel deposits at Porteau Cove, Furry Creek, and Britannia Beach are the result of the last ice age. A boulder-filled sand and gravel delta was formed by a stream when the sea level was 60 metres higher and the glacier in Howe Sound had partially melted.

Historic Britannia Mines

AT BRITANNIA BEACH, in contrast to other areas of the province, copper, not gold, was king. During the life of Britannia Mines, it produced 56 million tonnes of copper, enough to circle the globe in half-inch copper wire 12 times. Another 134 200 tonnes of zinc, 16 500 tonnes of lead, 14 million grams of gold and 84 million grams of silver were hauled out—in all, worth about $4 billion at today's prices. For many years, the mine at Britannia was the largest source of copper in the British Empire.

In 1888, Doctor Alexander Allen Forbes, a native of Aberdeen, Scotland, was tipped off to the area's rich copper deposits by a "dog fisherman" named Granger. Agreeing to pay Granger $400 if copper could be found, Forbes searched in the remote mountains. Just before sunset on the second day, a discouraged Forbes shot a deer. To his surprise, the animal's hooves revealed mineralized rock below the moss. Granger got his $400, bought a boat, and disappeared to Alaska.

Unfortunately, major capital was required to develop the relatively low grade copper. Unable to find an investor, Dr. Forbes moved on to discover a lucrative mine on Texada Island.

In 1899, an American mining

Mill No. 2 was started in 1913 and completed in 1916

engineer from Butte, Montana, visited the property. He convinced New York City financiers that the property had great potential. Access was from Britannia Landing and then along a 6-kilometre horse trail hacked through the dense forest to the mine at Jane Camp. An aerial tram was soon built to carry the ore down the mountain.

Almost overnight the bustling, isolated community of Britannia sprang up. The main townsite, originally called Jane Camp and later simply Townsite, was located high in the hills, next to the mine's entrance. It took 90 minutes to reach via aerial tram. A second townsite, the Beach, was developed near the shore. Another 40 families later lived at nearby Minaty Bay. Victoria Camp was located at Furry Creek near the present-day golf course. Eventually,

the mine was controlled by the Howe Sound Company, owners of the property for nearly 60 years.

The outside world came to Britannia Beach when the rail line was extended from Squamish to North Vancouver in 1956. Two years later, the Squamish Highway was completed. Community life could not compete with outside attractions, and the Townsite emptied after the mine was shut down for nine months. By 1959, the once-proud mine was reduced to seven employees and went into liquidation.

Anaconda kept the mine open until November 1, 1974. As the whistle blew a three-minute requiem, 55 men went underground for the last shift. In the 70-year life of the mine, 60,000 people called Britannia Beach their home.

When disaster struck

The outbreak of World War I increased the demand for copper. Prices rose sharply, and Britannia Mines invested $5 million in improvements to the mine and community. But the boom years were tempered by disasters.

Six kilometres up in the hills, at midnight on March 22, 1915, a landslide struck the Jane Camp townsite near the mine's entrance. After Alberta's Frank slide, it was the second most destructive landslide in Canadian history. Fifty-six people, including miners coming off the late shift, women, and children, were killed outright, 22 people were injured.

It was a terrible blow to the tiny, close-knit community.

Almost immediately, construction began on a new and safer residential area at the 670-metre level. Later, this area was called Mount Sheer or, simply, the Townsite. For permission to visit the old townsite, call Copper Beach Estates (896-2221). The walk from Britannia Beach, along the original road, takes three hours round trip.

The Jane Camp slide wasn't

Forces that shaped the land

THE GEOLOGICAL HISTORY along this route is fascinating; the forces that shaped the land are powerful and diverse.

The Coast Mountains are largely granite, cooled deep underground about 100 million years ago and eventually uplifted. Once exposed to the surface, the rising mountains began to erode. Streams cut deep, narrow valleys that were later widened by several ice ages. The last of these ice ages was 13,000 years ago, when a 1500-metre-thick glacier covered the area as far south as present-day Seattle.

When the ice retreated, the Squamish Valley had deepened. The rising sea level flooded its lower portion, creating Howe Sound. Especially hard rock withstood the onslaught to be polished smooth. No finer example exists than the Stawamus (Squamish) Chief, a monolith of granite created by the grinding and polishing action of rock carried by moving ice.

The processes that created the mountains and gave them their appearance continue to this day. The land is still rising over 1 centimetre every 100 years; erosion continues by a similar amount.

The Cinder Cone in Garibaldi Provincial Park

the end of Britannia's natural disasters. In October 1921, the beach community on the banks of Britannia Creek was destroyed by a massive debris flood. It came after days of heavy rain followed by an unprecedented 14.6 centimetres of additional rain that fell in a 24-hour period. To make matters worse, warm winds melted snow in the mountains. Nature was not entirely to blame—a culvert carrying the mine's railway over Britannia Creek got clogged with debris. Acting like a dam, it created a 60 000-cubic-metre lake. When it burst, a wall of water 21 metres wide and up to 1.5 metres high came surging down. Sixty houses were destroyed and 37 people were killed.

Teed-off

Golfers have their choice of more than half a dozen courses between Horseshoe Bay and Pemberton. Some have a track record of several decades;

After the tragic 1915 Jane Camp landslide, a new townsite was built above Britannia Beach. Now a ghost town, the Townsite can still be visited today.

Britannia Beach amenities and attractions

BY MINING STANDARDS, Britannia Beach was a stable community and a good place to live. The company store, for example, was a cooperative that supported community clubs. After the mine closed, Britannia Beach refused to die.

A small but active community of some 300 people continues to call Britannia Beach home. For a taste of true BC history, visit the BC Museum of Mining, then enjoy the galleries, restaurants, tearooms, gift shops, grocery store, and outdoor flea market the beach has to offer.

The BC Museum of Mining

Designated a national historic site, the BC Museum of Mining offers a guided tour into the mountain and has actual working displays. A gift shop and exhibit of rare photographs and artifacts round out the attraction. Visitors can also try their hand panning for gold—recovery guaranteed. Open May to September. For information on off-season hours and year-round prebooked tours, write Box 188, Britannia Beach, BC V0N 1J0. Or call 896-2233; toll-free from Vancouver, 688-8735.

The *Prince George*

Built in 1948, the MV *Prince George* now rusts quietly beside the Britannia dock. A veteran of summer sailings between Vancouver and Skagway, Alaska, the vessel was used as a floating hotel during Seattle's 1962 World Fair. A disastrous fire in 1975 caused more than $400,000 worth of damage. Sold in 1976 by the provincial government, the "Prince" was reborn as a floating restaurant in Nanaimo. Later, during the *Exxon Valdez* oil spill, the vessel served as a workers' residence in Alaska.

Today the forgotten prince of Britannia Beach awaits an undecided fate, requiring costly refitting before its next incarnation.

doors to others have recently opened. All are noted for their beautiful settings in Sea to Sky Country.

In Whistler, the Chateau Whistler Golf Club joined the race in 1993, 10 years after the opening of the Whistler Golf Club. A third club, designed by Jack Nicklaus, due to open in 1995, should confirm Whistler as an international golf destination. Competitive marketing makes for some good buys for visitors: ask about combination golf/accommodation packages.

Slowing the decline

No fish are more famous on the West Coast than BC salmon. Sadly, salmon, along with many other species, have suffered the effects of overfishing, habitat destruction, development, and pollution.

Attempts are being made, however, to build up what has been lost. Just past Brackendale, the Tenderfoot Hatchery, built in 1981, is one example. Its goal is to increase chinook salmon stocks in the Squamish River, in decline since the 1960s, when numbers dropped from some 25,000 fish to a mere 2000 in just two decades. The hatchery also enhances coho salmon and steelhead trout.

Hatcheries to visit and view Tenderfoot Hatchery:
North of Squamish off Highway 99. Take the Cheekye turnoff. Species: chinook, coho, and steelhead. The free-of-charge facility is open 365 days a year from 9:00 am to 3:00 pm. Visitors are invited to take a self-guided tour. Group tours may be arranged by calling 898-3657. Write Box 477, Brackendale, BC V0N 1H0.

Golf clubs enroute

GLENEAGLES GOLF CLUB
Located off Highway 99. Take Eagleridge exit to 6190 Marine Drive, Horseshoe Bay, 921-7353. Nine holes, first come/first served, no bookings, 2342 metres, dining, pro shop, view of Coast Mountains and Pacific Ocean.

Furry Creek Golf & Country Club
Off Highway 99 between Lions Bay and Squamish, 922-9576. Opened in 1993, 18 holes, 5852 metres, target-style course designed by Robert Muir Graves, clubhouse, panoramic views of mountains and seaside, canyons, forest, lake, creek.

Squamish Valley Golf and Country Club
A prestigious, semiprivate club located on Mamquam Road, turnoff at junction of Highway 99 and Mamquam, 898-9521; Pro Shop, 898-9691. Call for reservations. In operation for more than 25 years, 18 holes, restaurant, pro shop, curling, squash, near Mamquam River, view of mountains.

Whistler Golf Club
Opened in 1982, 18 holes, 5852 metres, par 72 course designed by Arnold Palmer, dining room, rolling greens, nine lakes, winding creeks, mountain views. Awarded *Golf* magazine Silver Medal in 1989. 932-4544; pro shop 932-3280.

Chateau Whistler Golf Club
Reservations, 938-8000; clubhouse office, 938-2092. Opened spring 1993, 18 holes, 66067 metres, par 72 course created by Robert Trent Jones II, side of Blackcomb Mountain, glacial streams, granite rock faces,

The Whistler Golf Club is one of half a dozen courses along Highway 99.

waterfalls combined with elevations of over 91 metres.

Green Lakes Golf Course
Whistler. Opening in 1995, Jack Nicklaus course. For more information, contact the Whistler Activity and Information Centre, 932-2394.

Pemberton Valley Golf and Country Club
Located near Pemberton Airport on Airport Road, 894-5122. 18 holes, mountain views, near Lillooet River. Senior's rates available.

Big Sky Golf & Country Club
Located in Pemberton at the base of Mt. Currie, 894-6106; toll-free, 1-800-668-7900. 18 holes, 6439 yards, par 72 course designed by Bob Cupp, restaurant, pro shop, golf academy, pastoral setting, views, 183 metres above sea level.

Other: Coastal Mountain Golf Adventures will book your golf tour. Box 1364, Whistler, BC V0N 1B0, 932-7998.

Gates Creek Project:
Operated by Dicor, a company wholly owned by the D'Arcy Indian Band, Gates Creek is located on D'Arcy Road past Mount Currie. Species: sockeye salmon. Displays explain the life cycle of sockeye; literature and a film, *Life of the Sockeye*, are available. Write De-partment of Fisheries and Oceans, General Delivery, D'Arcy, BC V0N 1L0.

Seton Creek Spawning Channels:
Operated under contract by local Indian bands. Seton Creek is located 5 kilometres from Lillooet beside Seton Creek. Species: pink salmon. Displays of life cycle of salmon; literature supplied with one week's notice. Pink salmon return every odd year. Write Department of Fisheries and Oceans, Box 1676, Lillooet, BC V0K 1V0.

Provincial parks at a glance

VISITS TO PROVINCIAL PARKS across BC topped 22 million in 1993. Numbers included 399,700 visitors to Shannon Falls, 96,000 back-country visitors to Garibaldi, and 717,274 visitors to the "Falls of '99": Shannon, Brandywine, and Garibaldi.

Along Highway 99, you'll enjoy the following BC Parks:

Porteau Cove Provincial Park:
25 kilometres north of Horseshoe Bay; 44 campsites. The park is divided into the diver's area, day-use area, campground area, and Porteau Cove itself. Scuba diving, boating, windsurfing, fishing, and hiking. The boat launch is the only one open to the public between Horseshoe Bay and Squamish. Firewood. Open year-round. For more information, see page 24.

Murrin Provincial Park:
3 kilometres north of Britannia Beach; 31 campsites. Browning Lake beside Highway 99; Petgill Lake by way of an 11-kilometre trail. Fishing, swimming, hiking, picnics. Popular with rock climbers.

Lake Lovely Water Recreation Area:
Turnoff at Brackendale. Access is by hiking trail only. Wilderness/walk-in sites.

Shannon Falls Provincial Park:
7 kilometres past Britannia Beach; no overnight camping; picnic area along Shannon Creek; toilets. A short walk takes you to the base of the 335-metre-high Shannon Falls. Established in 1984, Shannon Falls was originally a much smaller park. A larger section was acquired in 1990 to protect the site from logging.

Alice Lake Provincial Park:
13 kilometres north of Squamish; 95 campsites. Grassy meadows, forest trails, mountain views, bird-watching, canoeing, fishing, kayaking. For biking, the park's Four Lakes Trail is a gentle 6-kilometre climb and descent past four small lakes. Firewood. Open year-round.

Garibaldi Provincial Park:
Five entrances. 196 wilderness/walk-in sites. See more about Garibaldi Provincial Park on page 41.

Brandywine Falls Provincial Park:
34 kilometres north of Squamish; 13 kilometres southwest of Whistler; 15 campsites. Noted for its 70-metre waterfall, Daisy Lake, and views of the mountains of Garibaldi Provincial Park. Firewood. Open April-November. Nearby Calcheak Recreation Site is an overflow campsite.

Nairn Falls Provincial Park:
28 kilometres past Whistler, 3 kilometres south of Pemberton; 88 campsites; 171 hectares. The 60-metre Nairn Falls tumbles into the Green River. Pit toilets, drinking water, and firewood are available. Hiking, fishing for rainbow and Dolly Varden trout, and rafting down Green River are popular. Visitors can swim at One-Mile Lake, 2 kilometres north on Highway 99. Open April-October.

Joffre Lakes Recreation Area: On Duffey Lake Road, 32 kilometres from Pemberton, 71 kilometres from Lillooet. Wilderness/walk-in camping sites. Trail connects visitors to Lower, Middle, and Upper Joffre lakes. Be well prepared, equipped, and informed before entering the backcountry.

Duffey Lake Provincial Park:
A 2379-hectare park established in 1993. Located on Highway 99 roughly halfway between Pemberton and Lillooet. Scenic picnic spots; road access to the shores of Duffey Lake is limited. Boat launch site at east end. Former BC Forest Service campsite offers some camping areas, fishing, and hiking.

Birkenhead Lake Provincial Park:
90 kilometres north of Whistler; 85 campsites. Set amid snow-capped mountains, the park offers boating, fishing for kokanee and rainbow trout, and wildlife viewing. Firewood. Open May to late September.

For more information about local parks, call BC Parks Visitor Services at 898-3678.

Camping options

Camping enthusiasts enjoy hundreds of camping sites beyond Horseshoe Bay. In the Whistler/Garibaldi region alone, an area of 3700 square kilometres, 23 organized campgrounds and recreation sites, as well as dozens of wilderness walk-in sites can be found.

In addition to privately run campgrounds, overnight and recreational use along Highway 99 falls into four categories.

The best known are BC's provincial parks, established to preserve outstanding natural, scenic, historic, and recreational features. Some of the parks are in their natural state with no development, whereas others have facilities and are intensively used. The BC Parks office in Alice Lake can supply information and brochures.

Forest recreation sites are managed by the BC Forest Service, from which readers can obtain maps and information. Access and basic facilities are provided to maintain or enhance an area's recreation values. Low-key and rustic, they include outhouses and wooden picnic tables. Campers must supply their own firewood and drinking water. A free Forest Service recreation map detailing 16 recreation sites and 17 trails is available from the Squamish Forest District, 42000 Loggers Lane, Squamish, BC V0N 3G0; telephone: 898-2100.

Visitors may also camp in provincial recreation areas. In the Whistler/Garibaldi region, there are 17 such reserves. These have no developed facilities and are not actively man-

A variety of camping is available along Highway 99, including well-managed provincial parks

aged. Some do not have established access; get information from the BC Parks office.

Finally, there is Crown land, owned by the provincial government, also open for recreational use. This land is subject only to necessary closures and road restrictions.

Squamish

Whether you are looking for a good cup of coffee or the second largest granite monolith in the world to climb, Squamish is just the place. With a population of 12,000, it has traditionally made its livelihood in the logging industry—but tourism, recreation, and even filmmaking are making inroads where caulk boots once reigned.

Visitors along "the Corridor," as the locals call Highway 99, come by boat, train, and plane and overland. Under an hour's drive from Horseshoe Bay, the route is crisscrossed with creeks and graced with views of both Howe Sound and the peaks

and icefields of the Tantalus Range. For an even better view, tour the area by air. Glacier Air (683-0209), just outside Brackendale, includes a glacier walk in its flightseeing package.

Prevent forest fires

DO NOT SMOKE while walking. Stop for a smoke break.

1. Butt out on a rock or in the dirt and take your butt with you when you leave.
2. Use your ashtray, especially when driving on forest roads.
3. Respect fire closures and other restrictions.
4. Build campfires only in fire rings. No open fires are permitted.
5. Keep campfires as small as possible. Don't build a fire when winds are strong.
6. Tend your campfire at all times.
7. Extinguish your campfire completely before you leave the site.

Falls enroute

FALLS ALONG HIGHWAY 99

Depending on the season and the weather, dozens of glacier-fed waterfalls appear and disappear along Highway 99, coursing down steep, rocky slopes. Three year-round falls, the artwork of a period of glaciation ending 13,000 years ago, are now part of BC's provincial parks system.

Brandywine Falls

Located in Brandywine Falls Provincial Park, this 70-metre waterfall is not visible from the highway, but can be reached by following the signs to Brandywine Falls Provincial Park and walking 10 minutes from the parking lot to an observation platform on the canyon's rim.

Brandywine Falls Provincial Park is a popular weekend destination during the summer. There are a limited number of overnight camping spots. Many visitors take advantage of the day-use picnic area.

Shannon Falls

Located in Shannon Falls Provincial Park, established in 1984, Shannon Falls drops an impressive 335 metres. At its best in May when swelled by spring runoff, Shannon Falls is clearly visible from the highway.

Nairn Falls

Just 20 minutes north of Whistler, Nairn Falls is a fairly easy 1.5-kilometre hike from the parking lot along a trail beside the Green River. A narrow gorge squeezes the waters of the river into the falls, creating a powerful 30-metre-high

Brandywine Falls

waterfall that jogs three times before reaching bottom. After walking gingerly across granite slabs, you'll see the falls, often bathed in mist. Notice the potholes created by the friction of stones and gravel.

Shannon Falls

Nairn Falls

When the Pacific Great Eastern Railway pushed northward from Squamish in 1914, it proved a dream come true for the growing logging industry. Lumber and minerals from the BC Interior made their way down to Squamish, with foreign-made goods and machinery making the return trip. Logging progressed northward up the railway line until the watershed valleys were depleted. What you see as you drive along the highway is now second-growth forest.

An intense debate over the future rages in the Squamish Valley. Emotional as well as economic ties bind the community to logging. Clearcutting practices since the turn of the century have left both loggers and environmentalists questioning what will be left in 10 years. As a visitor, it's best not to broach the subject unless you're prepared for an earful.

Reform in the logging industry is happening slowly, but it is happening. In the meantime, Squamish is adjusting to new economic possibilities. The region's rock-climbing and windsurfing

Squamish, once known as Newport, is making a name for itself as a centre for outdoor adventure sports

areas are now internationally known. A recent survey, based on 14,859 windsurfing visits and 20,000 rock climber visits,

estimates that spinoff revenues from the two sports have pumped more than $2 million into the local economy.

Theft insurance

BC PARKS advises visitors to be extremely wary of theft from automobiles, particularly when hiking in to visit sites. To help prevent crime, observe the following guidelines:

Tip 1: Remove all valuables from your car.

Tip 2: Close all windows and lock all doors, even if your car is unattended for only a few minutes.

Tip 3: Leave the glove compartment open.

Tip 4: Auto burglar alarms are available. Advertise the fact that you have one with a window decal.

Tip 5: Stereos and CB radios are prime targets for thieves. Engrave your licence number on your possessions. Install them with removable brackets, allowing you to take them with you in areas of high risk.

Tip 6: If your vehicle doesn't have a locking gas cap, install one to

prevent vandalism or theft of gasoline.

Tip 7: Keep an inventory of all accessories with serial numbers for identification. Items commonly carried in your vehicle, such as tools, should be recorded by serial number.

Tip 8: Be a good citizen. If you see suspicious people in or around parked vehicles, call the police at 911.

If Vancouver is Hollywood North, then Squamish is definitely Hollywood Valley. Movies such as *K2, Medicine Man*, Sylvester Stallone's *Cliffhanger*, and *White Fang II* have all taken advantage of the valley's scenic beauty. Film sequences for the television series *MacGyver, Danger Bay*, and *Highlander* were shot on the Smoke Bluffs, a series of accessible crags that now compete with the Chief as a rock climber's magnet.

The streets of Squamish are pleasant to stroll, with cosy restaurants and good coffee shops. Mostly Books at 38071 Cleveland Avenue (892-3912) sells books by BC and other authors. Gift shops sell local arts and crafts, including Native wood carvings, jewellery, and prints. A small park adjacent to the Squamish Infocentre marks the spot where the Royal Hudson pulls in at noon, Wednesday through Sunday and holiday Mondays from June to mid-September. Drop by with a picnic lunch and watch as visitors disembark to tour the town.

The Sko-mish people

Before the European onslaught, the Coast Salish were a migratory people, travelling seasonally within their traditional territory to hunt, fish, gather food, and pick berries.

Spring and summer found them camping in shelters on the sound, such as those on Bowen and Anvil islands, and at Horseshoe Bay. In winter, they lived in longhouses in the Squamish Valley. They buried their dead in trees, and if possible, on an island. The Defence Islands across from Porteau Cove is a Squamish Nation burial site.

The Sea to Sky corridor runs the length of what is the northern territory of the Sko-mish (Squamish) Nation of the Coast Salish. Before the mid-1800s, Sko-mish villages extended from the south shore of Burrard Inlet, along Howe Sound and 100 kilometres up the Squamish River, as well as west to Gibson's Landing. Today Squamish territory includes Squamish, Chekwelp, Capilano, Seymour Creek, Mission (North Vancouver), Kitsilano, Port Mellon, and the Defence Islands.

Art work, carving, songs, and dances were, and are, part of Squamish daily life, and are an important means of teaching beliefs and kinship ties. As an elder from the Squamish Nation observed, "...our 'artistic' expressions are as much communication as they are 'art.'"

The Squamish were great traders inland and along the coast. Items included valuable mountain-goat wool blankets of Coast Salish weave and cedar basketry. Their weaving was finely crafted, as functional as it was beautiful. Carvings, basketry, and other works of art are now displayed and sold in many galleries and gift shops.

Squamish amenities

THE TOWN OF SQUAMISH offers a full range of amenities, including restaurants, accommodations, banking, gas stations, grocery and sporting goods stores, a liquor store, and a post office.

Maps

Maps are available from either of Squamish's Infocentres (downtown and Garibaldi Heights locations). A street map of Squamish may be purchased in the Infocentres or ordered from the Westport Publishing Co. Ltd., 302-895 Fort Street, Victoria, BC V8W 1H7.

You can also obtain maps at the Squamish Heritage Museum, located on 2nd Avenue in downtown Squamish. Contact the Squamish Valley Museum Society: 898-3273.

Special Days

May-June
• Royal Hudson Inaugural Run
• Sea to Sky Trade Fair

June
• SOAR Regatta
• Brodie Test of Metal Mountain Bike Race

August 1 long weekend
• Squamish Days Loggers Sports

September
• Cheakamus Challenge Mountain Bike Race

Accommodations
• Alpine Bed & Breakfast: 898-4306
• August Jack Motor Inn: 892-3504
• The Chieftain Hotel: 892-5222
• Dryden Creek Resorts: 898-9726
• Garibaldi Inn: 892-5204
• Gramma's Bed & Breakfast: 898-2063
• Klahanie Campground & RV Park: 892-3435
• Shannon's Bed & Breakfast: 892-3740

No life like it

In the early 1900s, it was the pole cutters who came into the Squamish Valley first, felling tall, straight trees for Vancouver telephone poles.

The first organized pole cutter in the area was a man called MacDonald. His camp, at the south end of Green Lake, supported a crew of men and a team of 15 horses. MacDonald cut poles all winter, skidded them down to the railway tracks, and shipped them out by the carload.

In 1917, a massive snowslide blocked the rail line and completely cut off the valley for six weeks. The loggers ran out of supplies and had to shoot their horses and walk out.

The valley went commercial in 1926. Three Barr brothers

Early BC loggers with a steam donkey used to pull logs from the bush

found a spot for a sawmill on the northeast corner of Green Lake. Logging camps sprang up, with as many as 200 men.

Companies also used steam donkeys, running along crisscrossing rail lines, to haul the logs to the booming grounds.

The way of change

NATIVE LIFE altered forever under European influence. When the Hastings and Moodyville sawmills opened in the 1860s in Vancouver, many Native people left their villages in Squamish for work. Native children were taken from their families and sent to residential schools. The 1880s brought smallpox, which quickly spread across the Squamish Valley. From 1876 to 1888, Native reservations along Howe Sound and Burrard Inlet were allotted and surveyed under the pressure of pioneering land development. A total of 26 reserves were assigned for the use of the Squamish people. In the early 1900s, 16 Squamish reserves amalgamated under the Squamish Indian Band.

Elders traditionally teach the younger generation

After decades of church and government control, the Squamish people today have regained their customs and traditions. These can be enjoyed and shared at powwows and other Native gatherings, many of which are open to the public.

Drop by the Squamish Nation's gift shop, located in the Native Cultural Centre beside Highway 99, south of the bridge over the Stawamus River and close to the Stawamus (Squamish) Chief. For more information, call 892-5166.

and proceed less than 1 kilometre. Visitors can also enjoy the Bluffs' hiking loop. A map beside the trail gives viewing points and approaches. Two outhouses are located here.

For more information on rock climbing and hiking in the area, contact the Federation of Mountain Clubs of BC, 336-1367 W. Broadway, Vancouver, BC V6H 4A9, 737-3053, or the Squamish Rockclimbers Association at 892-9662. Suggested reading is *The Rockclimber's Guide to Squamish* by local climbing pioneer Kevin McLane.

Squamish Valley bike trails

Bicycle enthusiasts can choose from easy to arduous in the Squamish Valley. Easy riding is afforded along the dyke trails of the Squamish Estuary. The flat backroads of the Squamish and Paradise valleys (turnoff

10 kilometres past Squamish) are also in this category. Above Alice Lake Provincial Park, cyclists find a wide variety of intermediate and advanced trails.

Even more challenging is the Sea to Sky Trail, under construction since 1993. An ambitious 300-kilometre bikeway linking Squamish with Seton Portage on the west side of Anderson Lake, the trail will be some years in the making. If you're up to it, try the section now complete from the sand sheds on Highway 99 at the north end of the Cheakamus Canyon. You'll bike 2.2 kilometres north past Deadman Lake to meet 8 kilometres of forestry road at Garibaldi Station on the BC Rail line. Hikers as well as bikers are welcome to try the trail. For more information, contact the Sea to Sky Trail Society, c/o Sea to Sky Enterprise Centre, Box 2539,

Squamish, BC V0N 3G0; telephone: 892-5467; Fax: 892-5227.

Highway 99 is already popular with cyclists. The very fit tackle the round trip from Squamish to Whistler in a day. For bike tours, contact Everything Outdoors Ltd., Box 415, Brackendale BC V0N 1H0, telephone 898-4199. For more on mountain biking in the area, see "Whistler in Summer."

Nature at your fingertips

Photographer Peter Timmermans knows the Squamish area well. With his trained photographer's eye, he's shot the mountains, rivers, and valleys of the area for the past decade. His favourite spot, he admits, may come as a surprise: a small field just north of Squamish that bursts into daisies every spring.

Nature's delights come in

Malibu on the Sound

THE NAME SQUAMISH means "Mother of the Wind" in Coast Salish, a testimony to the north winds that rise before noon and blow steadily until dusk. Winter winds—cold air funnelled from the Interior down the Cheakamus and Squamish valleys—can blow here with considerable force, averaging 40 knots an hour on the water with gusts as high as 70.

Squamish windsurfing is recognized as the best in Canada and in the top 10 in North America. Windsurfers have taken to the Squamish Dyke area at the mouth of the Squamish River in droves. While still in the works, under an estuary management plan, the windsurfing area would be designated a conservation

area. Long-term plans for the area include a beach, a race-viewing area, a grassy rigging area, a permanent shelter with change rooms and a first-aid station, a windbreak of trees, and a vehicle turnaround area.

Access is by way of Buckley Avenue and the fishermen's entrance. Visitors must angle-park on the right side of the dyke. A daily sailing fee of $10 is charged, with a season pass for $75. Spectators and nonsailing family

Windsurfers near Squamish

members are welcome at no charge. Proceeds help offset operating costs. For wind and event information, call the Squamish Windsurfing Society at 926-WIND (926-9463); this nonprofit society operates the sailing park and rescue service.

all sizes and shapes along Highway 99. There are three different forest zones. Below 900 metres is the coastal western hemlock zone. Coniferous trees here include the coastal western hemlock, western red cedar, and Douglas-fir. Black cottonwood, poplar, alder, and maple are common deciduous trees. Damp, shaded conditions promote a dense understorey of mosses, devil's club, and false Solomon's seal. Queen's cup, cow parsnip, starflower, and lilies are common flowers, along with wild rose, wild strawberry, and fireweed growing on disturbed sites.

Between 900 and 1550 metres, subalpine forests, including mountain hemlock, yellow cedar, Douglas-fir, and amabilis fir, dominate. Towards the treeline, the Douglas-fir disappears. Vegetation takes on a more open, parkland character. Clumps of trees, surrounded by shrubs, such as huckleberry, blueberry, and rhododendron, are scattered throughout numerous wildflower meadows.

At elevations above 1650 metres and in alpine meadows, the remaining conifers are stunted subalpine fir and whitebark pine. Displays of flowering plants highlight the alpine zone. Look for lupins, anemones, mimulus, penstemon, and phlox. Patches of low-growing plants, such as moss campion and saxifrage, are found among rocks in the subalpine tundra zone.

Garibaldi Provincial Park is noted for its extensive alpine meadows. Along with other smaller meadows to the west, these reach their peak of flowering brilliance in August. The Black Tusk meadows are the most famous. Singing Pass and Mamquam Lake are excellent above-treeline sites for viewing multicoloured alpine wildflowers.

Fine examples of massive trees can be found along the trails to Cheakamus Lake and to Nairn Falls. You'll see an outstanding stand of oldgrowth hemlock, fir, and cedar on the Cheakamus Lake trail. The large black cottonwoods that line the banks of the lower Squamish River are similar to those protected by the Baynes Island Ecological Reserve. The "Plus Tree" location on the Squamish River road has been set aside for recreational viewing by the Weldwood Company.

For more information, contact the Squamish Forest District, 42000 Loggers Lane, Squamish, BC V0N 3G0, telephone 898-2100. North of Whistler, contact the Pemberton Field Office (April-October), telephone 894-6112; Fax: 898-2191.

Brackendale, home of the bald eagle

Brackendale, one of the earliest settlements in the valley, predates even Squamish. Although the first settler here was a John Bracken, owner of the Bracken Arms Hotel (built in 1908, destroyed by fire in 1917), locals say the site was named for the wild bracken fern that grows here. Another pioneering family, the Thornes, settled north of today's Easter Seal Camp and established a hop farm. Many locals, including Native residents, worked there cutting hops. A row of hardwood trees where the Thorne farm originated can still be seen from Highway 99.

Brackendale today (population 1100) is noted for its annual bald eagle count. Also noteworthy is the Brackendale Art Gallery, Theatre & Teahouse, a mini-cultural centre created by sculptor Thor Froslev. It was Froslev who carved the eagle profile prominent on Highway 99 at the Brackendale turnoff.

The Brackendale Art Gallery Society, established in 1969, fosters indigenous art and artists. July through September, an exhibit of Pacific West Coast Native art features poles and carved figures, prints, masks, and beadwork from artists of the Squamish band.

Drop in for cappuccino and croissants, or book a dinner theatre show featuring gourmet meals made from locally grown produce. Upstairs is a gift shop with pottery, jewellery, clothing, and arts and crafts by BC artists.

Funding for the theatre comes from a number of sources. Throaty iron bells made on the premises are sold as a means of support. The Casting Wall, on the outside of the building, is another. For $100 and 30 minutes of your time, Froslev will cast your face in concrete and mount it on the outside wall.

The Brackendale Art Gallery, Theatre & Teahouse is open weekends and holidays, noon to 10:00 pm, or by appointment. Turn off Highway 99 at Brackendale, 10 kilometres past Squamish. Signs

Common West Coast trees

Douglas-fir (Pseudotsuga menziesii) Discovered in 1829 by Scottish botanist David Douglas, this widespread tree has been favoured as a Christmas tree and by loggers. Reaching heights up to 70 metres (but usually about 40 metres), with trunks to 90 centimetres in diameter, the Douglas-fir has flat, sharp, pointed but not prickly needles that look much like bottle brushes; needles stand out from three sides of the twig. The bark is thin, smooth, grey, and resin blistered when young, becoming deeply furrowed with dark reddish-brown ridges when mature. Douglas-fir is one of the best sources of strong, long-lasting timber used in construction, processed wood products, and the pulp and paper industry.

Subalpine fir (Abies lasiocarpa) Often erroneously called balsam fir, this true fir has a symmetrical, spirelike form. The trunk is slightly tapered and may be clear of branches for more than half of the tree's height. The branches are neatly whorled and slope downwards to withstand heavy ice and snow. The bark is grey and contains numerous resin blisters. Subalpine fir can grow to 50 metres in height but is often dwarfed and shrublike when found on exposed ridges at timber line. The wood is used for general construction and pulp.

Engelmann spruce (Picea engelmannii) Identify spruce needles by rolling them between your fingers. The four edges allow for easy rolling. (Be careful, because the tips are sharp.) The crown of a mature Engelmann spruce in the open is composed of wide-spreading branches at approximately right angles to the trunk. In closed stands, the tree is often clear of branches on its lower half. Because of low shrinkage and uniform texture, spruce is used for ladders, sashes, and frames.

Western red cedar (Thuja plicata) Another giant of the coast, Western red cedar grows to 60 metres tall and 2 metres in diameter. The frondlike branches are lacy and aromatic when touched. Cedar bark is thin and pliable, ideal for weaving into baskets, clothing, and mats. Totem poles, canoes, and lodges are carved from its wood. The trunk tapers from a fluted base up to a long, spiked top, which is often dead on mature trees. The wood is very light, free of pitch, and remarkably easy to split into boards or uniformly tapered "shakes" for roofing material. Western red cedar became British Columbia's official tree in 1988.

Ponderosa pine (Pinus ponderosa) This distinctive tree has a straight trunk topped by a loose mass of heavy branches with tufts of brushy foliage. In a hot, dry climate, it grows to an average height of 15 metres, but it can reach 30 metres. Needles, occurring in bundles of three, are yellowish-green with finely toothed edges. The bark on mature trees is orange-brown, with deep fissures dividing elongated plates. It is primarily used for sashes, frames, door mouldings, boxes, crates, cabinet work, and general construction.

Lodgepole pine (Pinus contorta) This tree is found almost everywhere in British Columbia, from the seashore, where it is called shore pine, to subalpine elevations, where it grows tall and lean.

Where its growth isn't stunted, Lodgepole pine grows to an average height of 20 metres. The crown is narrow and rounded, with the thin limbs often occurring only on the top third of the tree. The bark is mottled dark grey, with some trees showing light brown areas. It has a light covering of small loose scales. There are two needles to a bundle, often yellowish-green. The wood is largely used for railway ties, general construction, siding, and pulp.

point the way to Government Road. Telephone: 898-3333.

Regal roosts

British Columbia is blessed with almost half of the world's bald eagle population. A goodly portion of these make their winter homes in Brackendale. In 1994, the annual count was 3700 eagles, which may have exceeded the usual number at the Chilkat Reserve in Alaska, previously thought to have the world's largest number of bald eagles in one spot. Eagles come from as far away as Alaska, attracted by the runs of salmon in the Squamish River.

The first bald eagle count took place in Brackendale in 1985. Six people counted 500 eagles, and the event caught on. The count occurs in January during the annual Brackendale Winter

Nature's checklist

Trees
- ❏ Douglas-fir (coast)
- ❏ Western red cedar
- ❏ Coastal western hemlock
- ❏ Mountain hemlock (higher-elevation forests)
- ❏ Western white pine
- ❏ Sitka spruce
- ❏ Amabilis fir (higher-elevation forests)
- ❏ Western yew
- ❏ Ponderosa pine
- ❏ Western larch
- ❏ Engelmann spruce
- ❏ Willows (various species)
- ❏ Trembling aspen
- ❏ Paper birch
- ❏ White spruce
- ❏ Lodgepole pine
- ❏ Douglas-fir (interior)
- ❏ Yellow cedar (higher-elevation forests)
- ❏ Black cottonwood
- ❏ Red alder
- ❏ Subalpine fir

Berries
- ❏ Huckleberry (higher-elevation forests, near the treeline)
- ❏ Blueberry (higher-elevation forests, near the treeline)
- ❏ Elderberry (low-elevation forests)

Daisy field near Squamish

- ❏ Salmonberry (low-elevation forests)
- ❏ Strawberry (disturbed sites)

Herbaceous plants
- ❏ White rhododendron (higher-elevation forests)
- ❏ False azalea (higher-elevation forests)
- ❏ Salal (low-elevation forests)
- ❏ Ferns (low elevation forests)
- ❏ Hardhack (low-elevation forests)
- ❏ Ocean spray (low-elevation forests)
- ❏ Mosses (damp, shaded regions)
- ❏ Devil's club (damp, shaded regions)

- ❏ False solomon's seal (damp, shaded regions)
- ❏ Queen's cup
- ❏ Cow parsnip
- ❏ Starflower
- ❏ Fawn lily, glacier lily, Brodiaea, allium, fritillaries, and other lilies
- ❏ Wild rose (disturbed sites)
- ❏ Fireweed (disturbed sites)
- ❏ Rhododendron (near the treeline)
- ❏ Lupins (various)
- ❏ Anemone (alpine)
- ❏ Mimulus (various)
- ❏ Mimulus (monkey flowers)
- ❏ Penstemon (various)
- ❏ Phlox (alpine)

Eagle Festival hosted by the Brackendale Art Gallery, Squamish Estuary Conservation Society, and BC Wildlife.

Bald eagles, magnificent, long-worshipped birds of prey with wingspans in excess of 2 metres, are rare or endangered in most parts of North America—but not here. With an equally magnificent setting—the 2678-metre-high Garibaldi mountain as a backdrop—the bald eagles appear right at home.

Look for the eagles and their gigantic nests, called aeries, in the cottonwood trees in January and February. Bird watchers, hikers, photographers, and kayakers have a front-row seat on the dyke lining the Squamish River. Recommended spots are in front of the Lions Club's Easter Seals Camp on Government Road,

and farther north near Fergie's Cabins on Squamish Valley Road. One of the best places to see them is where the Cheekye River joins the Squamish River. To get there, turn left from the highway just north of Squamish and continue driving to the river.

Guided walks and kayak tours are also organized by Everything Outdoors, 898-4199. Viewing from the water puts you right at the eagles' dinner table as they dive for salmon. Kayaking also provides close-ups of seals, herons, cormorants, trumpeter swans, and the occasional golden eagle.

For more information on the annual event, contact the Brackendale Art Gallery, Theatre & Teahouse, Box 100, Brackendale, BC V0N 1H0, telephone 898-3333.

Garibaldi Provincial Park

Named in 1860 by British Royal Navy surveyor Captain George Henry Richards after Guiseppe Garibaldi, the 19th-century Italian hero and patriot, 2678-metre-high Mount Garibaldi is situated in

Garibaldi Provincial Park, an area of 195 000 hectares. A plaque honouring Garibaldi marks a pullout and viewpoint along Highway 99.

The Garibaldi Volcanic Belt is part of the Pacific Ring of Fire, an arc of volcanic activity from the tip of South America to Alaska and along the coast of Asia, including Japan and the Philippines. Mount Garibaldi last erupted 11,000 years ago. The south slope of the mountain, the original core of the volcano, is visible because much of the volcanic cone was built on a glacial ice sheet. When the ice retreated, the side of the mountain collapsed into the valley. A look at Garibaldi is a view into what is usually the hidden core of a volcano.

Even though nothing is erupting today, the result of molten eruptions is fascinating, especially where hot molten rock came into contact with cold glacial ice.

Between Mount Garibaldi and Black Tusk 2315 metres to the north lies the Barrier, a

Brackendale amenities

INCLUDE THE Brackendale Art Gallery, Theatre & Teahouse, an antique store, a grocery store, a café, and a post office.

Special Days
Winter:
    Brackendale Winter Eagle Festival
    Eagle Photo Contest
    Eagle Art Show
    Annual Eagle Count
    Eagle Photo Workshop
Summer:
    Pacific West Coast Native Art Exhibit. Brackendale Art Gallery, Theatre & Teahouse

300-metre-high cliff. Here again, ice and lava reacted, and the lava flowed until it was stopped by a particularly thick wall of ice. Later, water backed up behind the wall of rock to form Garibaldi Lake. Not visible from the highway is a formation called Cinder Cone, an almost-perfect flat-topped and steep-sided edifice. Cinder Cone was created when a volcano erupted underneath the glacial ice, which acted like a jelly mould to shape the molten rock.

The first recorded ascent of Mount Garibaldi was in 1907, by a party of six Vancouver climbers. The area quickly became a favourite destination for hikers, and in 1920, Garibaldi Provincial Park was created.

The park is large enough to offer numerous outdoor activities, including gentle hikes, camping, backcountry mountaineering, and Nordic skiing. Sights include frozen rivers of glacial ice, debris from volcanic activity, alpine meadows, wildlife, and birds.

There are five access routes into Garibaldi Provincial Park, all well marked. Progressing north on Highway 99, they are Diamond Head (4 kilometres north of Squamish, plus 16 kilometres to parking lot), Black Tusk/Garibaldi Lake (39 kilometres north of Squamish,

Garibaldi Provincial Park

3 kilometres to parking lot), Cheakamus Lake (56 kilometres north of Squamish, 8 kilometres to parking lot), Singing Pass (access is through Whistler Village, then

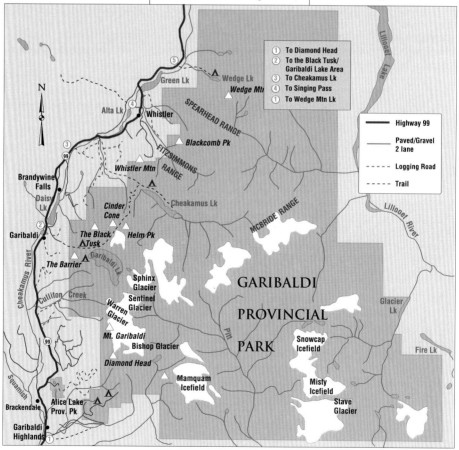

6 kilometres to parking lot), and Wedgemount Lake (8 kilometres past Whistler Village, 3 kilometres to parking lot).

After parking, be prepared to hike in to enjoy Garibaldi's more spectacular sights. No dogs or fires are allowed anywhere in the park. Bicycles are welcome only in the Diamond Head area from the parking lot to Elfin Shelter. A second bicycle area is the Cheakamus Lake Trail, Cheakamus access route.

For more information, contact BC Parks, Garibaldi/Sunshine District, Box 220, Brackendale, BC V0N 1H0, telephone 898-3678. Or drop by the Garibaldi/Sunshine District Office, located in Alice Lake Provincial Park. BC Parks publishes a very good map of Garibaldi.

Beware of bears

Considering the number of visitors to BC Parks, people/bear encounters are low. Attacks do take place, however, most resulting from careless actions and ignorance. A little knowledge can save your life.

Did you know...

- Black and grizzly bears both live in this region.
- Bears should not be fed, frightened, or harassed.
- Bears are not tame, gentle, or predictable.
- Bears generally go out of their way to avoid people.
- All bears are dangerous.
- Adult bears are strong. They can shred tents or damage recreational vehicles in pursuit of food.
- A bear is as fast as a racehorse.
- Bears have good eyesight and good hearing.
- Bears are strong swimmers, are agile tree climbers when young, and have an acute sense of smell.

Bear safety

WHEN IN BEAR COUNTRY, be a responsible camper and hiker. Keep all food and garbage out of reach in a tree cache or locked in your car trunk. Do not bury garbage; bears will dig it up and possibly revisit the site to become a danger to the next campers. Keep food away from sleeping areas; wear different clothes to sleep in from what you wore when cooking; avoid taking greasy, strong-smelling foods and fish on camping trips in bear country. Check with park staff. Watch your children and keep pets leashed. When hiking, stay with your group on designated trails. Watch for signs of bears such as tracks; droppings; overturned rocks; rotten trees; torn apart, clawed, bitten, or rubbed trees; bear trails; fresh digging; or trampled vegetation.

Above all, heed all posted warnings. Report all sightings and encounters to park staff.

If you spot a bear in the distance, make a wide detour and leave the area immediately. If the bear is at close range, do not approach it. Remain calm; keep it in view. Avoid direct eye contact. Back away safely and do not run.

If a bear attacks, a safe response depends on the species and whether the bear is being defensive or offensive. Bears sometimes bluff their way out of a confrontation by first charging, then turning away at the last moment. Generally, do nothing to threaten or further arouse the bear. Some experts suggest slowly putting your pack on the ground between you and the bear and then backing away. Many say, if nothing helps and the bear is upon you to roll into the fetal position and place your hands around your neck and head areas. Although fighting back may increase the intensity of an attack, it may also cause the bear to leave. Since bears are unpredictable, each incident is unique.

Recommended reading: *Bear Attacks: Their Causes and Avoidance* by Stephen Herrero (Piscataway, NJ: Winchester Press, 1985). For more information, contact BC Parks: 898-3678.

Whistler Resort

eeing is believing. After 100 kilometres of glittering Pacific waters and layers of coastal mountains, you reach Whistler Resort. Nature gives way to a bustling town, set against a backdrop of two internationally recognized mountains, Whistler and Blackcomb. Just three decades

ago, Whistler Resort was the dream of a few. Backcountry cabins marked the small community of Alta Lake, where condos and resort homes now

rise resplendent. Only the most devoted made the arduous seven-hour journey over rough BC Hydro access roads.

Whistler, an undeveloped

mountain named for the whistler marmot, obtained its first paved road in 1964, 50 years after the Pacific Great Eastern Railway (now BC Rail)

came through. Inaugural ski
runs followed in 1965. This mo-
mentous development was accomplished by the Garibaldi
Lift Company, later Whistler
Mountain Ski Corporation.
Franz's Run, named after
founder and first president
Franz Wilhelmsen, still exists.

Fifteen years later, Blackcomb Mountain opened its
doors. Today Whistler encom-
passes both Whistler and
Blackcomb mountains, run by
two friendly rivals, the Whistler
Mountain Ski Corporation and
Intrawest Development Corporation.

The area began as a sum-
mer resort, gaining promi-
nence for its winter activities.
Today there's a balance between seasons. Yes, you can
downhill and cross-country ski,
snowmobile—even snowshoe.
You can also drive, hike, fly,
bike, and canoe the area's
peaks and valleys.

And if sports are too arduous, stay close to Whistler.
More than 100 restaurants,
cafés, and pubs, great shopping, and a variety of live entertainment are offered winter
and summer. This superb region offers unlimited possibilities for recreation and leisure.

Over 5000 people now live
and work in Whistler year-

A hiking party relaxes on Black Tusk

round. The numbers swell to nearly 30,000 at peak times of the year. Some bemoan the loss of the old days, but there's no going back. When you're number one in North America, your aim—quite naturally—is to be number one in the world.

The start of it all

- **Pre-1850s:** The Pemberton Trail, travelled by Salish tribes for centuries, runs from Howe Sound to Lillooet. The Skomish (Coast Salish) hunt on the coastal side; Lil'wat people (Interior Salish) live inland. Alta Lake sits between the two

territories.

- **1855:** At Rubble Creek, a massive landslide roars down the Barrier, covering a thriving forest under several kilometres of rock and boulders. Heading north on Highway 99 (around kilometre 80), look for tree stumps on the far bank of the

Important numbers in Whistler

Whistler Activity and Information Centre: 932-2394
Whistler Central Reservations
Local: 932-4222 Toll-free from Vancouver:
664-5625.
Toll-free from BC/Canada/US: 1-800-944-7853; Fax: 932-7231
Whistler Resort Association
Administration Offices
4010 Whistler Way
Whistler, BC V0N 1B4
932-3928; Fax: 932-7231

Whistler Mountain Ski Corporation
Guest Relations
PO Box 67
Whistler, BC V0N 1B0
Toll-free from Vancouver:
664-5614
BC/Canada/US: 932-3434
Fax: 938-9174
Blackcomb Mountain Guest Relations
From Vancouver: 687-1032
BC/Canada/US: 932-3141

Blackcomb Hotel and Resorts Reservations
4557 Blackcomb Way
Whistler, BC V0N 1B4
932-2882
BC/Canada/US: 1-800-777-0185
Blackcomb Skiing Enterprises
4545 Blackcomb Way
Whistler, BC V0N 1B4
Toll-free from Vancouver:
687-1032
BC/Canada/US: 932-3141
Fax: 938-7527

Cheakamus River, exposed after years beneath rock and debris.

- **1858:** Hudson's Bay Company employees J. W. Mackay and Major William Downie are the first Europeans to travel the Pemberton Trail.
- **1859:** Gold rush on the Fraser River. Thousands of prospectors spill across the Bridge River Valley and Lillooet Lake area. Some stay on, building trailside cabins.
- **1860:** The steamer *Lady of the Lake* plies Anderson Lake, carrying prospectors and supplies.
- **1877:** The Pemberton Trail is upgraded by the BC government. After spending $38,000 on the project, the Howe Sound-Lillooet Cattle Trail, only a metre wide along rocky cliffs, is declared a failure.
- **1885:** Norwegians, the first European settlers in the Squamish Valley, are flooded out. They move to Bella Coola on the coast.
- **1888:** The first homes are built in the Brackendale area.

Myrtle Philip: Whistler pioneer

MYRTLE PHILIP was quite the woman. Decked out in ankle-brushing skirts of the pre-World War I era, she hiked, rode, and fished better than most men. Together with her husband, Alex, the 22-year-old Myrtle left Vancouver in search of untrammeled wilderness.

In 1912, when the Philips arrived at Alta Lake—the site of present-day Whistler—there was no road and no railway. The trip took several days, first aboard the ferry *Bowena* to Squamish, then on a bumpy two-horse buckboard stage to Brackendale. From here, equipped with tent and pack-horses, the Philips hiked along the narrow Cheakamus Canyon trail, over both the Cheekye and Cheakamus rivers. As you drive the canyon today, note how difficult the journey must have been.

The Philips finally reached Cheakamus Camp, a roadhouse 24 kilometres away. It was another day to Alpha Lake and John Millar's one-room cabin. Millar, an eccentric Texas-born cowboy, put up the Philips for $1.00 each, including room and board. Millar Creek Road in Whistler's commercial suburb, Function Junction, is named after this noteworthy pioneer.

The Philips later camped at Alta Lake, 1.5 kilometres north, the highest lake in the valley. In 1914, they opened Rainbow Lodge on the shore of Alta Lake, destined to become the most popular summer resort west of the Rockies. Along with the lodge, Myrtle ran a general store. For more than 30 years, she was also the postmistress.

People came to Rainbow Lodge to fish and enjoy the mountain air. They hiked, climbed mountains, and sailed. The Philips also kept saddle horses for the ever-popular activity of trail riding.

Myrtle, a great rider, angler and cook, died in 1985 at the age of 95. The Myrtle Philip Elementary School and recently opened Myrtle Philip Community Centre are named in her honour.

Sadly, Rainbow Lodge was destroyed by fire in 1978. Reminders of this bygone era,

Myrtle Philip could ride and fish with the best of them

including Myrtle's father's cabin and a replica of Alex Philip's famous Bridge of Sighs, remain at the Rainbow Park heritage site on the west side of Alta Lake.

*Compare the views riding
Whistler and Blackcomb
mountain chairlifts*

- **1902:** The Bracken Arms Hotel opens. Logging surpasses farming as the area's main industry.
- **1912:** Invited by backcountry cowboy John Millar, Alex and Myrtle Philip visit Alta Lake for the first time.
- **1914:** The Philips build Rainbow Lodge. The Pacific Great Eastern Railway pushes through from Squamish.
- **1920s:** Blackcomb Mountain is given its name by early settlers on the west side of Alta Lake. The cabin of early trapper and prospector Harry Horstman is located at 2256 metres, near today's Horstman Hut.
- **1926:** Commercial logging begins in the area.

- **1930s:** Rainbow Lodge is the premier summer resort west of Banff.
- **1948:** The Philips retire, remaining active in the community.
- **1958:** Hillcrest Lodge opens for two seasons.
- **1959:** Tyrol Ski Club is established on Alta Lake.
- **1960:** Lodges and sawmills share Alta Lake. Franz Wilhelmsen and others create the Garibaldi Olympic

What is Whistler Resort?

Entering Whistler:

Function Junction: A retail/industrial area 3 kilometres south of Whistler. Offers everything from cappuccino to Canadiana furniture to cellular phone sales and leasing.

"Home of the Downhill," Whistler Creek: Whistler Infocentre, accommodations, gas stations, shops, services, and access to Whistler Mountain. This was the original ski base.

Whistler Mountain: Opened in 1965. Ski from Whistler Village or Whistler Creek. In 1992, Whistler Mountain Ski Corporation invested $600,000 in trail development, removing 40 000 cubic metres of rock. Five kilometres of new trails resulted, serviced by Redline chair from Whistler Creek.

Whistler Village: Opened in 1980 around Village Square. Has hotels, restaurants, pubs, shops, the Whistler Conference Centre, banks, tour companies. Walk from Whistler Village to Blackcomb Benchlands in five minutes, crossing Fitzsimmons Creek.

Whistler Village North: Ten-year expansion of a 24-hectare site next to Whistler Village (Lorimer Road and Highway 99). Will double the size of the village. Opened or opening: condominium developments, shops, grocery store, liquor store, medical clinic, library, chapel, two hotels, three lodges, offices, recreation/cultural centre.

Whistler's Marketplace: A $25-million shopping plaza, front-runner in Whistler Village North development. Home to clothing, equipment, magazine, and book stores, as well as McDonald's, IGA food store, Toronto Dominion Bank. Future home of pharmacy, liquor store, post office, real estate offices.

Blackcomb Mountain: Opened in 1980. Since 1986, Intrawest has invested $70 million in mountain amenities. In 1992, Nippon Cable purchased a 23 percent interest for $25 million. Continued development includes the Excalibur high-speed gondola system.

Blackcomb Benchlands: Begun in 1982. Area around the base of Blackcomb Mountain. Includes a mix of hotels, shops, restaurants, condominiums, golf course.

Black Market: Blackcomb Benchlands' shopping area. Centered in and around Chateau Whistler and the base of Blackcomb Mountain.

Residential areas: Alta Lake Road, Bayshores, Whistler Creek, Whistler Highlands, Nordic Estates, Alta Vista, Blueberry Hill, Brio, Whistler Village, Whistler Village North, Blackcomb Benchlands, Horstman Estates, White Gold Estates, Nesters Square, Whistler Cay, Alpine Meadows, and Emerald Estates.

Blackcomb Mountain

A horsedrawn buggy creates a romantic interlude

Crowds mingle and meet in the Village

Whistler Mountain

Dining: choose between the great outdoors and gourmet

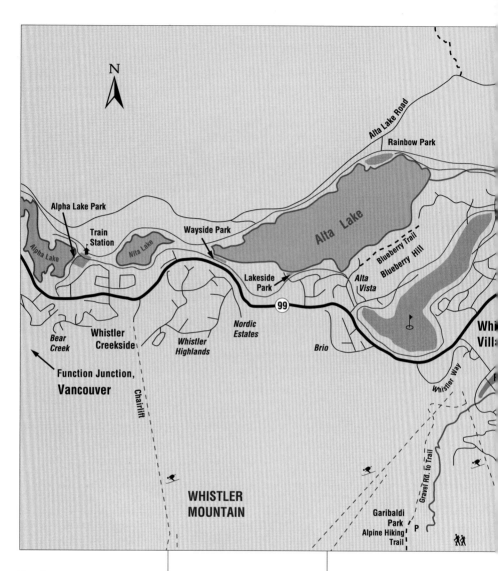

N

Alta Lake Road

Rainbow Park

Alpha Lake Park

Train
Station

Wayside Park

Nita Lake

Alpha Lake

Alta Lake

Blueberry Trail
Blueberry Hill

Lakeside
Park

Alta
Vista

99

Bear
Creek

Whistler
Creekside

Whistler
Highlands

Nordic
Estates

Brio

Whi
Vill

Function Junction,
Vancouver

Chairlift

Whistler Way

**WHISTLER
MOUNTAIN**

Garibaldi
Park
Alpine Hiking
Trail

Gravel Rd. to Trail

P

Development Association to develop the area's resort potential.

• **1964:** A paved road from Squamish is completed. Until now, the railway was the only link to Vancouver.

• **1966:** Franz Wilhelmsen's Garibaldi Lift Company opens Whistler Mountain's west side with the Red Chair gondola and two T-Bars on January 12. A double chairlift is soon added. London Mountain is renamed Whistler Mountain.

• **1974:** The BC government halts helter-skelter growth while a study is done.

• **1975:** The Resort Municipality of Whistler—British Columbia's first and only resort designation—is launched.

• **1976:** An official community plan is introduced. An alpine-style village with ski-in/ski-out access is set in motion.

• **1978:** Rainbow Lodge is destroyed by fire. Al Raine, ski coordinator for the BC government, puts out a proposal call for development of Blackcomb Mountain. Aspen Skiing Corporation invests in the project.

• **1980:** Blackcomb Mountain opens, doubling the area's ski capacity. Whistler Village opens; Whistler Mountain's northside follows with a high-

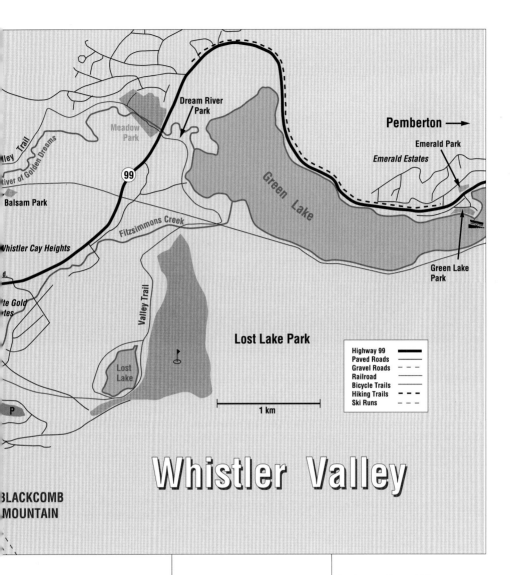

Highway 99 — Paved Roads — Gravel Roads - - - Railroad — Bicycle Trails — Hiking Trails - - - Ski Runs - - -

Dream River Park

Meadow Park

Pemberton →

Emerald Park

Emerald Estates

99

Green Lake

Balsam Park

Fitzsimmons Creek

Whistler Cay Heights

Green Lake Park

Valley Trail

Lost Lake Park

Lost Lake

1 km

P

Whistler Valley

BLACKCOMB MOUNTAIN

speed, 10-person gondola from the Village.

• **1986:** Intrawest acquires Blackcomb. The Peak Chair opens Whistler's high alpine bowls with 1521 metres of vertical.

• **1988:** Whistler Village gondola and three high-speed quad chairs are added between 1988 and 1991.

• **1991:** Whistler Resort earns its place as the number-one ski resort in North America. Blackcomb Hotels and Resorts' 452 condo/hotel suites begin construction.

• **1992:** Nippon Cable of Japan invests $25 million in Blackcomb lifts, snowmaking, and facility construction.

• **1994:** Excalibur, Blackcomb's $12.1 million high-speed gondola system, is introduced in November. Whistler's Harmony Express, a high-speed quad lift, is introduced in December. The resort is now rated number one in the world for high-speed lifts.

• **1995:** Whistler Village Centre opens in Whistler Village with hotel, shopping centre, restaurants. Underneath is the Whistler Adventure Club with 18-lane bowling alley, virtual reality centre, and billiards room.

Chateau Whistler Resort

A world-class resort

On its own, Whistler Mountain would be a great ski destination. Combined with Blackcomb Mountain, it's unbeatable. *SKI Magazine* and Japan's *Blue Guide Ski* both voted Whistler/Blackcomb one of the best places anywhere to ski.

Several years running, the influential *Snow Country Magazine* has rated Whistler the number-one ski resort in North America, competing against the top 50 resorts. According to *Snow Country*, "The tandem of Whistler and Blackcomb has the greatest vertical drop in North America, the most ski terrain, the most high-speed detachable quad lifts, and the most slopeside lodging."

Just as important are Whistler Resort's amenities. *Snow Country* named it the Best Overall Resort Design in its annual awards. The resort's continued success is due to its infrastructure, notably shopping and recreational opportunities. Nouveau European architecture blends plazas, walkways, shops, restaurants, lounges, and a wide variety of accommodations.

What makes Whistler the best:

• The largest ski area on the continent: more than 2792 hectares of skiable terrain, over

---

The top 10 ski resorts

BEING ONE OF the top 10 resorts in North America is no easy feat. *Snow Country Magazine* uses a point system to rank resorts in eight categories: vertical drop, patrolled skiable area, days of operation, expert acreage and percentage, number and types of lifts, beds within 400 yards (366 metres) of a lift, natural snowfall, and snowmaking coverage. Fifty percent of the score is based on the reports of 7000 readers on more than 20,000 separate visits. Rating the resorts, 1993/94:

1. Whistler/Blackcomb: 93.95
2. Vail, Colorado: 91.05
3. Squaw Valley, California: 88.28
4. Killington, Vermont: 87.50
5. Mammoth Mountain, California: 86.75
6. Heavenly Valley, California: 86.31
7. Steamboat, Colorado: 85.80
8. Aspen, Colorado: 84.48
9. Breckenridge, Colorado: 82.77
10. Park City, Utah: 82.49

200 trails, 10 alpine bowls, including 3 glaciers.
- The two greatest vertical rise ski mountains in North America, with Blackcomb Mountain rising one vertical mile (1600 metres) and Whistler Mountain 1530 metres.
- Fast access to the alpine from three separate mountain bases, all five minutes from each other, all equipped with high-speed lifts.
- The most extensive high-speed lift system in North America; 9 express lifts, including 1 gondola and 8 quad chairs, in a system of 28 lifts.
- Ski-in, ski-out convenience from Whistler Village, Blackcomb Benchlands, and Whistler Creek.

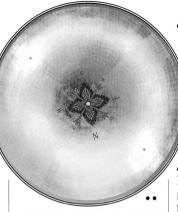

•• *Gold leaf painstakingly painted on a domed ceiling in the Chateau Whistler*

- Average annual snowfall of 9.14 metres, complemented by extensive snowmaking systems.
- Season running from November through May. Summer skiing until August.

- Distinctive shops, restaurants, lounges, and nightclubs.
  - Other winter activities from cross-country skiing, ice skating, and sleigh rides to paragliding, snowmobiling, and heli-skiing.
    - Warm, friendly service.

Accommodations

Finding a room in Whistler needn't be daunting. Over 60 hotels/condos provide over 2700 rooms. Choices range from basic bed in dorm-style lodges, pension-type inns, and bed and breakfast establishments to high-end accommodations such as the Chateau Whistler Resort.

All areas, including Whistler Village, Blackcomb Benchlands, and Whistler

Nancy Greene Raine

NO NAME is more synonymous with Whistler Resort than Nancy Greene, Canada's multi-medal Olympic champion. Together with husband and former Canadian national ski team coach Al Raine, Nancy Greene Raine continues to be a winner—at the community level—in Whistler Resort, where she lobbied for community-based projects such as the Whistler Health Care Centre and the recently opened emergency care facility complete with a heli-pad for mountain rescue.

Everywhere you travel in BC, you'll see Nancy's accomplishments celebrated. Near Rossland, BC, her home town, Nancy Greene Provincial Park, Nancy Greene Recreation Area, and Nancy Greene Lake commemorate her awards: two world cups, in 1967 and 1968, and Olympic gold and

Nancy Greene Raine: Canadian Olympic medalist

silver medals in 1968 at the age of 24. At Grenoble, her 2.7-second margin in the Giant Slalom was one of the widest in Olympic history.

Shortly after, Nancy retired and married Al Raine. In the late '70s and '80s Al and Nancy were instrumental in the development of Whistler Resort. Much of Whistler's

success can be attributed to Al's vision of what Whistler could become, and his tenacious lobbying combined with Nancy's enthusiastic promotion helped get the resort through the difficult early years. In 1985 they built Nancy Greene's Olympic Lodge, which quickly became one of the most successful in Whistler. In 1988, the Raines sold their hotel to Japanese investors and it was renamed Nancy Greene Lodge, with Nancy actively involved in management. The hotel was recently re-sold and is now operating as Crystal Lodge.

The Raines recently set out to conquer a new mountain. Nancy is now director of skiing at Sun Peaks Resort Corp. near Kamloops; Al is executive director of the Sun Peaks Resort Association.

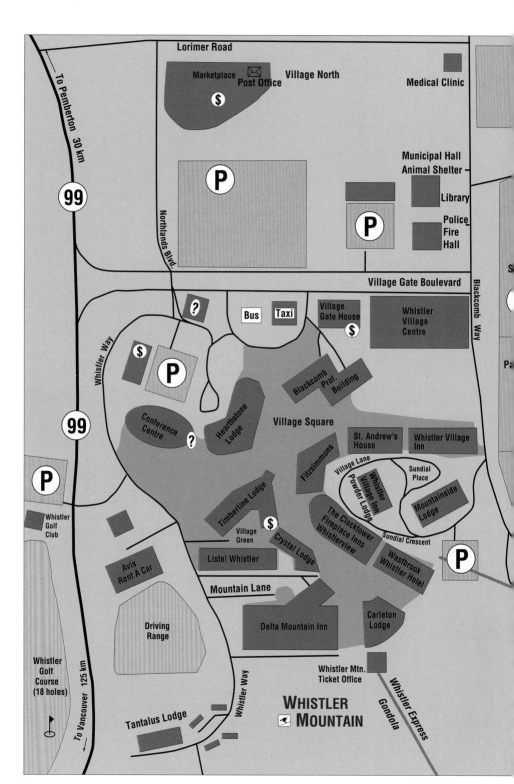

Lorimer Road

Marketplace
Post Office
Village North
Medical Clinic
$

Municipal Hall
Animal Shelter
Library
Police
Fire
Hall

P

P

To Pemberton 30 km
99

Northlands Blvd.

Village Gate Boulevard

Blackcomb Way

?
Bus Taxi
Village Gate House
$
Whistler Village Centre

Whistler Way
$
P
Conference Centre
?
Hearthstone Lodge
Village Square
Blackcomb Prof. Building

St. Andrew's House
Whistler Village Inn

Fitzsimmons
Village Lane
Whistler Village Inn Powder Lodge
Sundial Place
Mountainside Lodge

Timberline Lodge
$
Village Green
Crystal Lodge
The Clocktower Fireplace Inns Whistlerview
Sundial Crescent
Westbrook Whistler Hotel
P

99
P
Whistler Golf Club

Listel Whistler
Mountain Lane

Avis Rent A Car

Driving Range

Delta Mountain Inn
Carleton Lodge

Whistler Golf Course (18 holes)

125 km

Whistler Way

Whistler Mtn. Ticket Office

WHISTLER
MOUNTAIN

Whistler Express
Gondola

Tantalus Lodge

To Vancouver

56

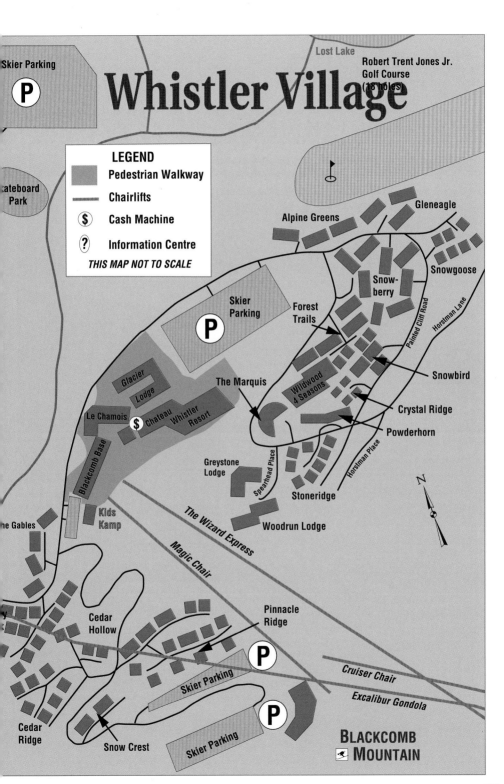

Whistler Village

Skier Parking

P

Lost Lake

Robert Trent Jones Jr. Golf Course (18 holes)

LEGEND

Pedestrian Walkway

Chairlifts

$ Cash Machine

? Information Centre

THIS MAP NOT TO SCALE

Skateboard Park

Alpine Greens

Gleneagle

Snowgoose

Snow-berry

Painted Cliff Road

Horstman Lane

Skier Parking

P

Forest Trails

Glacier Lodge

The Marquis

Wildwood 4 Seasons

Snowbird

Le Chamois

$ Chateau Whistler Resort

Crystal Ridge

Powderhorn

Horstman Place

Blackcomb Base

Greystone Lodge

Spearhead Place

Stoneridge

The Gables

Kids Kamp

The Wizard Express

Woodrun Lodge

N

Magic Chair

Cedar Hollow

Pinnacle Ridge

P

Cruiser Chair

Skier Parking

Excalibur Gondola

P

Cedar Ridge

Snow Crest

Skier Parking

BLACKCOMB MOUNTAIN

Creek, offer a wide selection of condominiums and hotel apartments. Slopeside properties are defined as those less than a five-minute walk to lifts.

Rates vary over the course of a year. In general, Early Value (November 24-December 17) and Late Value rates (March 27 onward) are lowest. Christmas rates (December 18-January 1) are highest. January rates (January 2-27) drop slightly, rising for the Regular rate period (January 28-March 26). Dates for Regular, January, Value, and Christmas seasons may vary according to property. Provincial sales tax and the 7 percent Goods and Services Tax are not included in quoted rates. Non-Canadian visitors qualify for a Goods and Services Tax (GST) rebate on

Accommodation rental companies

- Alpine Vacation Accommodation Whistler: 938-0707; Fax: 938-1061
- Blackcomb Hotels and Resorts: 932-2882/ 1-800-777-0185
- Crown Resort Accommodations: 932-2215/ 1-800-565-1444; Fax: 932-2266
- Four Seasons Vacation Rentals: 932-3252; Fax: 932-2579
- Juniper Hill Property Management: 932-8719; Fax: 932-8719
- Mountain Resort Accommodations: 938-3369
- Northern Comfort Accommodations: 932-5403; Fax: 932-5250
- Powder Property Management: 932-8700; Fax: 938-1888
- Rainbow Retreats: 932-2343
- Sea to Sky Leisure: 932-4184/1-800-688-8864; Fax: 938-9611
- Whiski Jack Resorts: 932-6500/1-800-944-7545; Fax: 932-6533
- Whistler Chalets and Accommodations: 932-6699/ 1-800-663-7711
- Whistler Exclusive Property Management: 932-5353; Fax: 938-3410

- Whistler Resort Management: 932-2972; Fax: 932-2756
- Whistler Sportpak International: 938-1184
- Wildflower Exclusive Accommodations: 932-4113; Fax: 932-4486

Hotels/lodges
- Blackcomb Lodge: 932-4155/1-800-777-8146; Fax: 932-6826
- Brew Creek Lodge: 932-7210; Fax: 932-7223
- Chateau Whistler Resort: 938-8000/-1-800-268-9411; Fax: 938-2055
- Carleton Lodge: 932-4183; Fax: 932-4101
- Clocktower Hotel: 932-4724; Fax: 932-4258
- Crystal Lodge: 932-2221/1-800-667-3363; Fax: 932-2635
- Delta Mountain Inn: 932-1982/1-800-268-1133 (Canada)/1-800-877-1133 (US)
- Fairways Hotel: 932-2522
- Fireplace Inns: 932-3200; Fax: 932-2566

Whistler offers a full range of accommodations

- Glacier Lodge: 938-3455
- Greystone Lodge: 932-2888/1-800-777-0185; Fax: 932-2882
- Hearthstone Lodge: 932-4161/1-800-663-7711; Fax: 932-6622
- Lake Placid Lodge: 932-4184/1-800-565-1444; Fax: 938-2913/932-2266

accommodations.

Consider a rented log chalet for a large group. Privately owned, and run by experienced property managers, chalets sleep up to 12 people with luxury amenities, including whirlpool tubs, large beds, down quilts, and landscaped private yards.

Probably the easiest way to book a hotel room, studio, studio/loft, chalet, or condominium is through Whistler Central Reservations, which covers many of the accommodations listed. In Canada and the US (except BC) call toll-free 1-800-WHISTLER (1-800-944-7853); 664-5625 in BC; direct 932-4222; Fax: 932-7231. Other booking agencies are listed below.

Accommodation rental companies

- Le Chamois: 932-8700/ 1-800-777-0185; Fax: 938-1888
- Listel Whistler Hotel: 932-1133/1-800-663-5471; Fax: 932-8383
- Marketplace Lodge: 938-6699
- Marquise: 938-1484/ 1-800-777-0185; Fax: 932-2882
- Mountainside Lodge: 932-4511/1-800-777-8135; Fax: 932-6864
- Ravencrest: 932-2215/ 1-800-565-1444; Fax: 932-2266
- Southside Lodge: 932-2554
- Tantalus Lodge: 932-4146/ 1-800-268-1133 (Canada); 1-800-977-1133 (US); Fax: 932-2405
- Westbrook Whistler: 932-2321/1-800-661-2321
- Whistler Creek Lodge: 932-4111
- Whistler Fairways Hotel and Resort: 932-2522/ 1-800-663-5644; Fax: 932-6711
- Whistler Resort & Club: 932-5756; Fax: 932-2969
- Whistler Timberline Lodge: 932-5211/1-800-663-3473
- Whistler Village Inns: 932-4004/1-800-663-6418; Fax: 932-3487
- Wildwood Lodge: 932-3252;

Fax: 932-2579

Timeshare/resort clubs
- Intrawest Resort Club: 938-3030; Fax: 938-9281
- Whiski Jack Resorts Ltd.: 932-6500/684-6592/ 1-800-944-7545; Fax: 932-6533
- Whistler Vacation Club: 932-6999; Fax: 932-6444

Pension inns/ bed & breakfast inns
Private rooms with complimentary breakfasts in Whistler homes
- Alpenhaus Wohlgemuth: 932-3588; Fax: 263-8193
- Alpine Lodge: 932-5966; Fax: 932-1104
- Alta Vista Chalet: 932-4900; Fax: 932-4933
- Brio Haus: 932-3313; Fax: 932-4945
- Canada West Bed & Breakfast Reservations: 932-2755; Fax: 929-6692
- Carney's Cottage: 938-8007; Fax: 938-8023
- Chalet Beau Sejour: 938-4966; Fax: 263-7825
- Chalet Luise: 932-4187; Fax: 938-1531
- Durlacher Hof Pension: 932-1924; Fax: 938-1980
- Edelweiss Pension: 932-3641; Fax: 938-1746
- Golden Dreams Bed & Break-

fast: 932-2667/ 1-800-668-7055
- Haus Stephanie: 932-5547
- Haus Heidi Pension: 932-3113; Fax: 932-4116
- Highland House: 898-3334; Fax: 898-3334
- Idylwood Bed & Breakfast: 932-4559
- Rainbow Creek: 932-7001
- Stancliff House: 932-2393
- Swiss Cottage: 932-6062

Alternate choices
Contact the following directly.
- BCIT Club Lodge: 932-4660
- Fireside Lodge: 932-4545
- Rod's Mountain Chalet: 932-2754
- Shoestring Lodge: 932-3338; Fax: 932-8347
- UBC-AMS Whistler Lodge: 932-6604/822-5851
- Whistler Youth Hostel: 932-5492
- Whistler Campground and RV Park: 932-5181

Dining

Food at Whistler is one of the great bonuses. From breakfast to late-night dining, the resort offers an almost overwhelming choice. Over 80 restaurants, cafés, bistros, pubs, specialty food shops, and fast-food outlets vie for the privilege of feeding over a million visitors annually.

If you're not the muffin-and-coffee-to-go type, breakfast is served from 6:00 am onward. On the slopes, Fresh Tracks, a buffet breakfast combined with first access to Whistler Mountain, is offered daily.

Many skiers consider breakfast an appetizer to lunch, when the real hunger kicks in. Everything from snacks to full lunches is available on Whistler and Blackcomb slopes.

For a warm-up java, try Blackcomb's Rendezvous (at the top of the Solar Coaster) or Horstman Hut (top of Seventh Heaven). Christine's at Rendezvous Ridge is perfect for sit-down dining with a view of Wedge Mountain and Armchair Glacier.

Blackcomb's Glacier Creek alpine restaurant also offers 360-degree views. A 15-metre glass wall encircles a space for 1000 diners. Upstairs is the River Rock Grill (750 seats; West Coast fare); downstairs is the Bite, a take-away counter. A 300-seat barbecue patio is part of the complex. Glacier Creek is located at the base of Jersey Cream and Glacier Express quad chairs.

On Whistler Mountain, Pika's (pronounced pee-ka's) looks sharper these days, thanks to a $3.6 million renovation and expansion. Offering cafeteria-style food, it now seats 1000 people. For full-service meals, there's the Roundhouse (next to Pika's, top of Whistler Express Gondola) and Raven's Nest (top of Quicksilver).

If après-ski on the patio is your choice, try the Longhorn (base of Whistler Village) or Dusty's Den (Whistler Creek, Quicksilver base). Citta, in Whistler Village Square, and

---

Profile: Lori Ternes

EVERY JANUARY, Chateau Whistler chef Bernard Casavant and his herb grower, Lori Ternes, have a seed meeting. After culling through her continent-spanning collection of catalogues and taking a tally of seeds she's saved from previous years, they determine the direction Chateau Whistler kitchens will take for the following year.

"Chili peppers are important," says Lori, owner of Mount Currie's Lillooet Lake Herbs and Flowers, "and I grow tons of basil, including cinnamon, Thai, and lemon basil." Basil seeds are supplied by California's Shepherd's Seed. One of Canada's most eclectic growers, Saltspring Island Seed, provides a variety of dried beans. "Because Bernie wants colour, I'm growing both Jacob's Cattle and kidney beans," adds Lori.

Lori's vivid mesclun salad

Lori Ternes

mixture contains white-stemmed and ruby chard, red orach, mache, sharp-leafed mizuna, Japanese red and green mustards, various endives, kales, and raddichios, all grown in her garden on Lillooet Lake Road, just past Mount Currie. Shungiku, Chinese chrysanthemum leaves and flowers, also find their way into her salads, as does purple perilla. Few growers have such variety, and still fewer deliver personally.

Lori's amazing garden results from living in the Pemberton Valley, known as the Banana Belt of BC. Growing here is not without its perils, however. After Lori spent five years building up sandy soil, a flood washed away the entire garden. "Nature's way of keeping one humble," says Lori. She started over. In addition to supplying several gourmet restaurants with fresh greens, Lori also sells dried flowers to florists and the public at Mount Currie's farmers market.

Having grown up near Vancouver, Lori has lived in the Mount Currie area for more than a decade. Other secrets of success are her husband, Fraser Andrew, a former chief of the Mount Currie band, and two sons, Robert and Jason, all of whom help in the garden. For more information, call 894-6508.

the Savage Beagle also offer après-ski fare.

Dinners off mountain come with pasta, tapas, and sushi. Choose from Mediterranean, Tex/Mex, French, Continental, Japanese, Chinese, Greek, Italian, and more. For dining suggestions, see next page.

Whistler's bars and clubs number more than 30. Some offer live entertainment; others, tapas. Most have television sets to catch sporting events.

For dining suggestions, see next page.

Avoid being towed

IF YOU PARK ILLEGALLY, your car will be towed away. Fees of more than $65 are charged. At the same time, the Whistler Towing company is handy if you lock your keys in the car or need a jump start on a cold morning.

To avoid being towed:
- Pay close attention to parking signs in and around the Village.
- Be especially careful to avoid fire lanes.

To retrieve a towed car, follow Village Gate Boulevard to Blackcomb Way. Turn left. Watch for Whistler Village Parking on right. Whistler Towing's yard is located left of parking lot, before the Lost Lake Trail.

Whistler services

Health/medical services
- Gateways Dental Clinic: 938-1550
- Whistler Creek Orthopedic & Sports Physiotherapy Clinic: 932-4203
- Whistler Dental Office: 932-3677
- Whistler Health Care Centre: 932-4911
- Whistler Medical Clinic: 932-3977
- Whistler Physiotherapy: 932-4001

Chiropractors
- Dr. Robert J. Hasegawa: 932-1922
- Dr. Ralph Schmidt: 932-3106

Dentists
- Dr. James C McKenzie: 932-3677
- Dr. John S. Roberts: 938-1550

Eye physician/surgeon
- Dr. Elliot Frankelson: 932-3687

Optical
- Mountain Optical (24 hours): 932-2904

Optometrist
- Dr. Karen Smith: 932-2600

Physicians
- Dr. Rob Burgess: 932-3977
- Dr. Elizabeth Crosby: 932-4404
- Dr. James DeMarco: 932-3977
- Dr. Ernest Ledgerwood: 932-4404
- Dr. Christine Rodgers: 932-3977
- Dr. Ron Stanley: 932-3977

Physiotherapists
- Whistler Physiotherapy: 932-4001
- Creekside Physiotherapy: 932-4203

Animal clinics
- Coast Mountain Veterinary Services: 932-5391
- WAG (Whistler Animals Galore): 932-4499

Travel agents
- Roseway Travel: 938-0111; Fax: 938-0112
- Young's Travel Service: 932-5757; Fax: 938-9486

Gas stations
- Husky Gas: 932-5715
- Petro-Canada: 932-6222

One-hour photo
- Slalom (1HR) Photo: 938-8006
- Whistler One Hour Photo: 932-6612/932-6676

Groceries
- Food Plus: 932-6193 (24 hours)
- The Galloping Grocer Deliveries: 932-6222; Fax: 932-5633
- The Grocery Store: 932-3628; Fax: 932-3679
- Husky Store & Deli: 932-3959
- McKeever's General Store: 932-3600
- Nesters Market: 932-3545; Fax: 932-3542
- Shop for You: 938-3274; Fax: 938-3278

Beer and wine
- Blackcomb Beer & Wine Store: 932-9795
- Whistler Brewing Company: 932-6185. Retail store and tours

Campground
- Whistler Campground and RV Park: 932-5181. Two kilometres north of Whistler on Highway 99

Local publications
- *The Whistler Journal*: 932-6500; Fax: 932-6533. Tabloid newspaper, published four times a year
- *Whistler, The Magazine:* 932-5131; Fax: 932-2862. Appears seasonally. Glossy look at Whistler and its people
- *Whistler Question:* 932-5131; Fax: 932-2862. Weekly newspaper; appears Thursdays

Whistler Mountain:
932-3434

Several restaurants are located on Whistler Mountain. They include the Roundhouse (top of Whistler Express Gondola), offering full-service meals; Pika's (top of Whistler Express Gondola) a cafeteria-style restaurant; Raven's Nest (top of Quicksilver), also cafeteria-style with pasta, salads, and a spacious deck. Located at the Whistler Creek Base (base of Redline Quad) are Quicksilver Café and Dusty's.

Blackcomb Mountain:
932-3775

Blackcomb's on-mountain restaurants include Horstman Hut (top of Seventh Heaven), a cafeteria-style restaurant with homemade goulash and soups. At the top of Solar Coaster Express are the cafeteria-style Rendezvous; Christine's Restaurant, with gourmet meals in a dining-room setting; and the Mountain Grill, with Mexican-style food plus burgers and pizzas.

Crystal Hut (top of Crystal Chair) is a log cabin serving stews, chili, and soups. Glacier Creek (base of Glacier Express) features the River Rock Grill, with international fare and a cappuccino bar. The Bite offers bistro-style service and foods.

Off the mountain in the Blackcomb Daylodge are the Wizard Grill for breakfasts, cappuccinos, and lunches, and Merlin's après-ski bar.

Other places to dine:
American Cuisine

• Jimmy D's Roadhouse: 932-4451. Across from the Whistler Fairways Hotel. Gourmet burgers, chicken, ribs, pasta, steaks.

Big screen at Jimmy D's Sports Bar. Daily; breakfast to dinner.

• Johnny's Grille: 932-3531. Carleton Lodge. American cuisine. Daily; lunch and dinner.

• Keg at the Mountain: 932–5151. Keg Lodge. Salads, steak, seafood. Adjacent to Brandy's Lounge. Daily; dinner.

• Monk's Grill: 932-9677. Base of Blackcomb Mountain. Prime rib, steak, seafood. Daily; lunch and dinner. Lively bar.

• Peter's Underground: 932-4811. Whistler Village. Cafeteria-style family restaurant. Free delivery. Daily; 6:30 am to 11:00 pm.

Asian cuisine

• Amami: 932-6431. Westbrook Whistler Hotel. Ramen, Japanese, and Chinese cuisine. Ski in for lunch, après-ski, dinner daily.

• Irori: 932-2221. Crystal Lodge. Japanese dishes; sushi bar. Open from 4:00 pm, 7 days a week. Reservations recommended.

• Sushi Village: 932-3330. Westbrook Whistler Hotel. Japanese cuisine. Dinner daily; lunch Sunday to Wednesday. Reservations for four or more recommended.

• Sushi Village Too: 938-0078. Le Chamois, Resort on Blackcomb. Daily; dinner. Reservations recommended.

• Teppan Village: 932-2223. Delta Mountain Inn. Japanese cuisine prepared at your table. Daily; dinner. Lunch Sunday to Wednesday.

• Whistler Garden: 938-9781. Delta Mountain Inn. Chinese cuisine. Daily; dinner. Takeout available.

Continental cuisine

• The Border Cantina: 932-3373. 1.5 kilometres north of Whistler Village on Highway 99. Southwestern/Thai cuisine. Daily; breakfast and dinner. Reservations recommended.

• Evergreens Restaurant: 932-1982. Delta Mountain Inn. Pacific-Northwest cuisine. Adjacent to Cinnamon Bar, with satellite TV, pool tables, dart board. Daily; breakfast to dinner.

• Florentyna's/Hoz's Pub & Café: 932-5940/ 932-4424. 2129 Lake Placid Road, Whistler Creek. Fresh pasta, seafood, ribs. Adjacent pub. Daily; dinner. Reservations recommended.

• La Rua Restaurante: 932-5011. Main level of Le Chamois, Resort on Blackcomb. International menu; Spanish. Daily; breakfast and dinner. Weekends for lunch. Reservations recommended.

• Myrtle's: 932-5211, ext. 106 Timberline Shops Mall. Daily; dinner. Reservations recommended.

• O'Douls Restaurant/Lounge: 932-1133. Listel Whistler Hotel.

Steaks; fresh seafood. Daily; breakfast and dinner. Reservations recommended.

- Oyster Bar: 932-5565. Highland Lodge, Whistler Creek. Fresh seafood. Daily; dinner. Reservations recommended.
- Rim Rock Café & Oyster Bar: 932-5565. Highland Lodge, Whistler Creek. Daily; dinner. Reservations recommended.
- Timberline Restaurant: 932–5211, ext. 106. Timberline Shops Mall. Daily; dinner. Reservations recommended.
- The Wildflower: 938-2033. Chateau Whistler Resort. Fresh seafood. Daily; breakfast to dinner. Sunday brunch. Reservations recommended.

French cuisine

- Chez Joël: 932-2112. Whistler Village Square. Continental cuisine, fondues. Adjacent bar. Daily; lunch and dinner. Sunday brunch available. Reservations advised.
- Les Deux Gros: 932-4611. Two kilometres south of Whistler Creek on Alta Lake Road. Daily; dinner. Reservations recommended.
- Val d'Isere: 932-4666. Upstairs, St. Andrew's House. Daily; lunch and dinner. Reservations recommended.

Greek cuisine

- Zeuski's Taverna: 932-6009. Mountain Square, next to Whistler Express. Open daily for lunch and dinner.

Italian cuisine

- Il Caminetto di Umberto/Umberto's Lounge: 932-4442. Whistler Village. Adjacent lounge with entertainment some evenings. Daily; dinner. Reservations recommended.

- The Original Ristorante: 932-6408. Westbrook Whistler Hotel. Takeout and delivery. Daily; dinner. Lunch weekends and holidays.
- Settebello's: 932-3000. Whistler Creek Lodge, Whistler Creek. American and Italian cuisine. Daily; dinner.
- Trattoria di Umberto: 932–5858. Mountainside Lodge. Daily; lunch and dinner. Reservations recommended.

Mediterranean cuisine

- La Fiesta: 938-2040. Chateau Whistler Resort. Tapas bar. Spanish Mediterranean cuisine. Daily; from 5:00 pm. Entertainment.
- Ristorante Araxi: 932-4540. Whistler Village Square. Northern Mediterranean cuisine, Italian cuisine West Coast-style. Pasta, game, wine cellar, pastries. Adjacent bar. Daily; lunch and dinner. Reservations recommended.

Pub fare

- Citta: 932-4177. Whistler Village Square. Pub fare. Daily; lunch and dinner, 11:00 am to 1:00 am.
- Longhorn Pub: 932-5999. Carleton Lodge. Pub fare. Daily; lunch and dinner. Entertainment.
- Tapley's Pub: 932-4011. Across from Whistler Conference Centre. Pub fare. Daily; full menu to 10:00 pm.

Tex-Mex cuisine

- The Border Cantina: 932-4246. Shoestring Lodge, 1 kilometre north of Whistler Village. Daily; dinner.

Delis/Cafés/Bistros

- Café a la Mode: 938-0378. Westbrook Whistler, Mountain

Square. Daily; 7:00 am to 5:00 pm.
- Chalet Corner Deli: 932-8345. St. Andrew's House, Whistler Village. Daily; 8:00 am to 6:00 pm. Indoor seating.
- Glacier Café: 932-7051. Glacier Lodge, Resort on Blackcomb. Daily; 7 am to 5 pm. Indoor seating.
- Hoz's Pub Café: 932-4424. 2129 Lake Placid Road, Whistler Creek. Daily.
- Ingrid's Village Café: 932-7000. Whistler Village. Daily; 7:30 am to 6:30 pm. Indoor seating.
- Mad Café: 932-6666. Whistler Village. Daily; 8 am to 10 pm. Indoor seating.
- Moguls Coffee Beans Co: 932-4845. Beside Pharmasave, Whistler Village. Daily; from 7 am. Indoor seating.
- Whistler Gourmet: 932-3949. Across from Whistler Conference Centre, Whistler Village. Daily; from 7 am. Indoor seating.
- Whistler Cookie Company: 932-2962. St. Andrew's House, Whistler Village. Daily; from 7 am. Indoor seating.

Fast food

- A & W: 938-9165. Bank Building. Hamburgers. Daily; 8:00 am to 10:00 pm.
- Misty Mountain Pizza Co.: 932-2825. Bank Building. Daily; 11:00 am to 3:00 am. Second location, Function Junction: 938-3200.
- Southside Deli: 932-3368. 2102 Lake Placid Road. Breakfast served 6:00 am to closing at 3:00 pm.
- Subway: 932-3244. Bank Building. Submarine sandwiches. Daily; 10:00 am to midnight.

SHOPPING IS PART of many a great holiday. Whistler is made for shoppers, offering quality sportswear and evening wear, ski gear, equipment, locally made gold and silver jewellery, pewter, pottery, and country crafts. Good shopping shoes are a must: there are over 80 stores to browse through, seven days a week.

Areas to explore:
Whistler Village

- Basic & Beyond: 932-6664. Home accessories, bonsai.
- Berg and Berg: 932-3856. (Crystal Lodge); 932-2374. Barbarian rugby jerseys, sweatshirts.
- Boutique Yokohama: 932-3038. Unusual fashions, bags, skincare.
- Brick Shirt House: 932-5320.
- Can-Ski-Village: 938-7755. Ski wear, hard goods, boot fitting.
- Carlbergs Gifts: 932-3554. European and casual fashions, gifts, stationery.
- Christmas at Whistler: 932-3518. Everything you need for Christmas decorating.
- Club Monaco: 932-3457. Casual weekend wear.
- Country Cottage: 932-2525.
- Creations & Delights: 932-4672. Paintings and pottery.
- Delta Works: 938-0113. Sports shirts, sweaters, accessories.
- Durango Boutique: 932-6987. Western clothes, jackets, boots, jeans.
- Escape Route: 938-3338. Out-

Winter and summer, Whistler is a shopping mecca

door fashion and equipment.
- Fun for Kids: 932-2115. Clothing, shoes, toys for infants to age 14.
- For Keepsakes: 932-3900. Sterling silver earrings, pins.
- For Nature's Sake: 938-9453. Nature-inspired gifts, books.
- Forget-Me-Nots: 932-3939.
- Great Games & Toys: 932-2043. Playthings, pastimes.
- Home on Deranged: 932-6650. Hand-painted clothing, antique watches.
- Inside Out Boutique: 932-2145. Lingerie, swimwear, activewear, hosiery.

- International Boutique: 932-1278. Affordable jewellery, watches.
- Jayeson Goldsmithing: 932-6341 Custom-designed jewellery.
- Laughing Stock Gifts: 932-3554. Birthday gifts, party supplies, gag gifts.
- McConkey's Sport Shop: 932-2391/932-6712/ 932-2311.
- June Country Shop: 932-3038. Pillows, birdhouses, cookbooks.
- Locals Casual Wear: 932-6013.
- McCoo's: 932-2823. Sports accessories for adults and children.

- Memories of Whistler: 932-6439. Sheepskin slippers, sweatshirts, Frederick Remington bronze replicas.
- Mountain Gallery: 932-5001. Works by BC artists.
- Mountain Moments: 932-3274.
- The Mountain Shop: 932-2203. Camping and climbing equipment, trail food.
- MuchoMacho: 932-6445. Old West cowboy hats, boots, belts, Navajo-style jackets.
- The Northwest Connection: 932-4646. West Coast artists' jewellery.
- Polo Ralph Lauren: 932-6127. Signature classics.
- Rocks and Gems: 938-3307. Crystals, stones, costume jewellery.
- Roots: 938-0058. Genuine Canadian leather goods.
- Rumpleshirtskins: 932-2040. Village Square.
- Seasons: 932-1954. Outerwear, denim shirts, sweaters.
- Shades of Whistler: 932-2298.
- Shepard Gallery: 938-3366. Canadian and international art.
- Shirtprint Originals: 932-2550.
- Snowberries: 932-3778. Baskets, bouquets, wind chimes, mugs.
- Sport Style: 932-6409. Casual wear, accessories for men and women.
- Sports West: 938-7777. Ski rentals, clothes, ski repairs.
- Sportstop: 932-5495. Sports outfitters.
- Symington's: 938-0223. Lingerie.
- Tokyo-do Gift Centre: 932-5495.
- Terri-O: 938-1948. Weekend wear.
- Village Traditions: 932-4438.
- Waves Co.: 932-4248.
- Whistler Clothing Co.: 932-7004. Separates, accessories.

- Whistler Gifts: 932-1970.
- Whistler Gifts & Sports: 932-1918.
- Whistler Hardware: 932-3863. Hardware, games, toys.
- Whistler Tops: 932-3910.
- Whistler Village Art Gallery: 938-3001. Glass, sculpture, ceramics, woodwork.
- Whistler Village Sports: 932-3327. Sporting goods and equipment.

Blackcomb Benchlands

In and around Chateau Whistler. Includes the Black Market, one of Whistler's newest shopping areas, located at the base of Blackcomb Mountain adjacent to Chateau Whistler. Shops include:
- Berg & Berg: 932-2374. Quality sportswear, specializing in tops.
- Blackcomb Ski & Sport Shop: 938-7788. Fashions and accessories, ski equipment, snowboard rentals.
- Blackcomb Treasures: 932-6609.
- Can-Ski-the-Glacier Shop: 938-7744. Hard goods, boot fitting, ski wear, children's wear.
- Excess: 932-2224. Sports accessories, bicycle and Rollerblade rentals.
- Forget-Me-Nots Gifts and Souvenirs: 938-3433. Magazines, books, novelty items, teddy bears.
- Gaauda Native Fine Arts: 932-3382. Paintings, sculpture, jewellery, furniture.
- Glacier Shop: 932-5709.
- The Golf Shop: 938-2021. Golf equipment, accessories, sweaters.
- Horstman Trading Co.: 938-7725. European ski wear and fashions.

- Memories of Whistler: 938-9459. Sheepskin slippers, sweatshirts, Frederick Remington bronze replicas.
- Monod Sports: 938-2017. Fine-quality sportswear
- MuchoMacho: 938-6445. Old West cowboy hats, boots, belts, Navajo-style jackets.
- Open Country: 938-9268. Handcrafted Canadian sweaters, footwear, classic casuals.
- Pacific Shirt Company: 938-9444. Original Canadian fashions in nylon and polar fleece.
- Picadilly Place: 938-1625. Gifts, magazines, newspapers.
- Snowflake: 938-2019. Canadian designer fashions, specialty knits, leathers, accessories.
- Van Raniga Jewellers & Designers: 938-1100. Award-winning jewellery designs.

Whistler's Marketplace
- Beautiful British Columbia: 932-0240. BC magazines and souvenirs.
- Durango 2: 938-0983. Casual clothes, men's denim, jeans, boots.
- Escape Route: 938-3228. Outdoor fashion and equipment.
- Great Games & Toys: 932-2043.
- Westbeach: 932-2526.

Function Junction
- Funky Junk: 938-4959. Alternative clothing, crafts.
- Loral Furniture and Fine Woodworking: 932-1211. Furniture and fine woodworking.
- Judi's Antiques: 938-1055. Antique pine Canadiana.
- Kathmandu: 932-6381. Consignment sporting goods.

Whistler in Winter

Whistler Resort is number one in North America for two very good reasons: Whistler and Blackcomb. On these two side-by-side mountains, skiers enjoy more than 2800 hectares of skiable terrain and more than 1600 metres (a mile!) of vertical drop. The continent's largest high-speed lift system, servicing three mountain bases, whisks skiers to the top.

Ten bowls, 3 glaciers, and more than 200 trails—steep alpine chutes, challenging mogul fields, secluded tree skiing, novice slopes, vast backcountry, great snowpack, Nordic skiing, and groomed cruiser runs—are all here for skiers' enjoyment.

Each mountain has its own brand of ski experience. From Blackcomb's sky-high runs to Whistler's wide-open bowls, the high-alpine skiing is unsurpassed in North America and rivals the major ski resorts in Europe.

Three mountain bases (Whistler Village, Blackcomb Base, and Whistler Creek), all equipped with high-speed lifts, assure fast access to the alpine. In the 1994/95 season, new high-speed lifts opened 3100 acres of exceptional terrain.

Growing space

Since opening in 1965, development has continued apace in Whistler. Today more than 1.3 million winter visitors swell the mountain during the ski season. Whistler Mountain's 1993/94 season set a record with 665,000 skiers, an increase of 15 percent over the previous year. Blackcomb's skier visits topped off at a record 789,884, exceeding the previous record of 764,500 skier visits the year before.

The resort saw increased

Riding the quad chair at Blackcomb

Mountain now add up to more than 760,000 a year. Consider that in 1985/86, Blackcomb's total was only 278,000.

As even the briefest of visits proves, Whistler and Blackcomb mountains don't rest on their laurels. Both have invested multimillions in recent years in upgrading, improvements, development, and strong marketing campaigns.

Snow, the basic ingredient, plays its part. In the 1993/94 season, Whistler Mountain recorded a snowfall of almost 12 metres at its midmountain weather station. During one 24-hour period, 82 centimetres fell on Blackcomb Mountain.

And when it's raining down below, remember that the locals say, "It's clear above 1000 feet." Both mountains have daily snow reports, available by telephone. You'll also

numbers of visitors from the UK, Germany, Australia, New Zealand, Japan, and the US. Good press such as being named the number-one ski resort in North America and high-profile events such as the World Cup downhill all help.

Blackcomb's nickname is "the Mile-High Mountain." Skier visits on Blackcomb

Faster and higher

THE LIFT COMPETITION continues between Whistler and Blackcomb mountains. A case in point is the Excalibur versus Harmony Express challenge.

In November 1994, Blackcomb launched Excalibur, a gondola system of 82 eight-passenger sitdown cabins capable of carrying 2500 skiers an hour.

Leaving Whistler Village, Excalibur climbs 454 vertical metres in less than eight minutes to the base of a new high-speed quad chair at the bottom of Honeycomb Run. Glacier Express lifts off at the base of Jersey Cream Bowl, passes over sheer rock cliffs, spans the Horstman Glacier twice, and crosses over the top of the Glacier T-Bar.

Turnaround times to Blackcomb and Horstman glaciers and high alpine areas are reduced by 50 percent. Glacier Express all but eliminates lift lines on the Seventh Heaven Express. All in all, a formidable engineering feat to the tune of $13.5 million.

In December 1994, a brand new high-speed detachable quad chairlift began operations on Whistler Mountain.

In less than six minutes, Harmony Express whisks skiers from the mountain's former Blue Chair base to the top of Little Whistler Peak. Vertical rise is 522 metres over a distance of 1772 metres.

At the top lies 485 hectares of skiing and snowboarding, including four bowls: Harmony Bowl,

Glacier Bowl, Symphony Bowl, and Sun Bowl. If you want to go even higher, link up with the Peak Chair, which vaults you up a cliff face and onto the Peak Lookout.

Lift capacity is 2400 per hour, increasing Whistler Mountain's high alpine capacity by 250 percent. This terrain is best tackled by intermediate or advanced skiers.

A total of $6 million has been invested in the lift and new trail work, including a widened and lowered access to Glacier Bowl and an intermediate run from the top back to Pika's restaurant. Two new snowcats are also in evidence.

find daily updates on snow conditions posted throughout the resort.

SOME SAY Whistler Mountain is easier for beginners; others that Blackcomb Mountain is. You decide. Study the mountains, ski the more than 200 trails.

Get to know the mountains by taking a ski lesson. Instructors guide you while you get up to speed, from Blackcomb's longest beginner run, Mainline (8 kilometres), to Whistler's most challenging routes in its West and Whistler bowls.

Let it snow

THE SKI SEASON at Whistler is one of the longest anywhere. Both Whistler and Blackcomb mountains officially open in late November. Whistler's ski season runs to late April; Blackcomb's to late May. Blackcomb reopens for summer glacier skiing from mid-June to mid-August.

Whistler's average annual snowfall is an abundant 9.14 metres/30 feet/360" on the summits. Yet Highway 99 is snow free 90 percent of the time.

For mountain snow conditions, call:

Blackcomb Mountain Snow Report
• Vancouver: 687-7507
• Whistler: 932-4211

Whistler Mountain Snow Report
• Whistler: 932-4191
• Vancouver: 687-6761

BC Ministry of Highways Road Information Service.
• Vancouver: 525-4997
• Abbotsford: 855-4997
• Whistler: 938-4997
• Kelowna: 860-4997
• Kamloops: 371-4997
• Victoria: 380-4997
• All other BC areas: 1-800-663-4997

Road trouble?
• BC Automobile Association 1-800-663-2222 (toll free)
• Whistler RCMP: 932-3440;

Emergency
• 932-3044

Whistler Mountain
• Opened: 1966
• Top elevation: 2182 metres
• Base elevation: 652 metres
• Vertical: 1530 metres
• Terrain: 1480 hectares
• Terrain type: 25% novice; 55% intermediate; 20% advanced/expert
• Lift capacity: 22,815 skiers per hour
• Lift system: Ten-person high-speed gondola, 4 high-speed quad chairlifts, double chairlift, 3 triple chairlifts, 1 T-bar, 2 handle tows
• Snowmaking: 40 hectares
• Number of trails: 100+ marked runs

Call or write:
Whistler Mountain Ski Corporation
PO Box 67, Whistler, BC V0N 1B0. Telephone toll-free from Vancouver: 664-5614, 932-3434; Fax: 938-9174

Whistler Activity and Information Centre
Located in the Whistler Conference Centre, 4010 Whistler Way, Whistler, BC V0N 1B4. Drop by/call 932-2394

Reservations
Whistler Resort Association Central. Located in the Whistler Conference Centre, 4010 Whistler Way. Whistler, BC V0N 1B4. Telephone: direct: 932-4222; Vancouver: 685-3650. Toll-free (US/Canada except BC): 1-800-944-7853

Blackcomb Mountain
• Opened: 1980
• Top elevation: 2284 metres
• Base elevation: 675 metres
• Vertical rise: 1609 metres
• Terrain: 1352 hectares
• Terrain type: 20% novice; 55% intermediate; 25% advanced/expert
• Lift capacity: 27,112 skiers/hour
• Lift system: Eight-passenger gondola, 6 high-speed detachable quad chairlifts (1 covered), 3 triple chairlifts, 2 T-bars, handle tow
• Snowmaking: 120 hectares
• Number of trails: 100+ marked runs

Call or write:
Blackcomb Skiing Enterprises
4545 Blackcomb Way, Whistler, BC V0N 1B4. Telephone: 932-3141; Fax: 938-7527. From Vancouver: toll-free 687-1032

Reservations
Blackcomb Hotels and Resorts 4557 Blackcomb Way Whistler, BC V0N 1B4 932-2882/toll-free (North America) 1-800-777-0185

Blackcomb

Whistler

BOTH WHISTLER and Blackcomb mountains offer extensive ski programs. Terrain from gentle slopes to wide alpine bowls allows instructors to provide lessons from tots to seniors, beginner to expert, individuals to groups. Lessons for skiers with disabilities are also available. For programs for children and youth 12–16 years, see "Whistler for Kids."

For more information on the mountains, contact:

- Guest Relations, Whistler Mountain Ski Corporation. Box 67, Whistler, BC V0N 1B0. Telephone: 932-3434 toll-free from Vancouver: 664-5614; Fax: 938-9174
- Blackcomb Ski School. 4545 Blackcomb Way, Whistler, BC V0N 1B4. Telephone: 938-7720; toll-free from Vancouver: 687-1032; Fax: 938-7527

Whistler Ski School

A variety of skiing programs is available on Whistler Mountain, including snowboarding. Lessons are offered from first-time skier (Level 1) to expert (Level 9) as well as for children and youth (12–16). For children and youth ski programs, see "Whistler for Kids."

Class lessons

- Full-day and half-day lessons allow instructors to introduce a range of Whistler Mountain's terrain and focus on skiing goals.
- Half-day lessons are offered for skiers of every ability from first-timers to expert. All half-day lessons are available with lift, lesson, and rental packages. Half-day clinics for small groups of similar ability, provid-

Expert instruction provides maximum skiing enjoyment

ing individual attention, are also available. Clinics include Parallel Improvement, Bump Clinic, and Powder Clinic.

- Other classes include the All-Day Cruiser Class and Gate-busters (for skiers with previous racing experience).

Multiday programs

- Cantel Dave Murray Masters Ski Camp: Three-day camps. Strive for maximum improvement with some of the best coaches in the country. Slalom, giant slalom, video analysis, on-hill snacks, atomic demo skis, and lots of free skiing.

Adult Adventure Ski Camps

- Two-day weekend camps. Video analysis, après-ski recep-

tion, technical supplement, and line priority on the Peak Chair. Check the Ski School brochure for dates.

Women Only

- The original women's program by Stephanie Sloan. Gates, bumps, and powder; snowboarding for beginners and low-intermediate riders. Maximum class size: 8. Video analysis and gourmet picnic included in program.

Frequent Skier Specials

- For early-season skiers. Video-analysis, technical supplement.

Skis schools offer instruction for all levels

Blackcomb Ski School

Blackcomb Mountain's ski school, voted one of the top five ski schools in North America by *Outside Magazine*, is the largest in North America, with more than 200 instructors. Lessons are offered for eight ability levels: Beginner/Novice (5 levels); Advanced/Expert (3 levels). Children and teen lessons also available. See more in "Whistler for Kids."

Class lessons

Full- and half-day lessons for all levels. A dedicated beginner chair and slope get you safely started. Intermediates and experts get personalized instruction.

All-day clinics challenge intermediate and advanced skiers while introducing the mountain's vast alpine terrain. Clinics include Cruiser Club (intermediate) and Super Class (advanced to expert). Workshops include Parallel Perfection, Bump, and Powder.

Multiday programs

• Five-Day Lesson Package offers five consecutive days of unlimited access to group lessons, workshops, and all-day clinics.

Excel programs

Patent-pending Excel series of pre-registered, multiday programs that focus on specific skills. They include the following:

• Kathy Kreiner's Perception Ski Workshop: For intermediate and advanced skiers seeking

Helpful hints

HALF-DAY LESSONS provide a minimum of two hours of teaching time.

• Give yourself 40 minutes for selecting rental equipment before starting your lesson.
• Wear warm clothes, a hat, gloves, and sunglasses or goggles.
• If you are meeting friends at the end of a lesson, confirm where you'll finish.
• ID is required in the rental shop.
• Pre-registration is recommended.

expert status. Olympic gold medallist and sport psychologist Kathy Kreiner blends skiing technique with confidence-building exercises.

• Ladies Unlimited: Women-only program, coached by former Olympian Judi McIntosh. Learn positive new techniques, banish fears, and see real improvement. Three- and four-day programs or weekend course.
• Greg Athans's Mogul Camps: Former two-time world champion Greg Athans combines video analysis and technical instruction to improve skiing on bumps and steeps.
• Mountain Masters: For men only, intermediate level. Small groups learn bumps, powder, steep-skiing tactics, and strategies.
• Felix Belczyk Ski Camps: Improve skiing technique or racing form. Canadian Olympic team member and World Cup Champion Felix Belczyk offers two- and three-day technical camps.

Both mountains

• Skiing for people with disabilities: Individual ski lessons are taught by specially trained instructors. Visiting skiers can use outriggers and a sit ski. Contact the mountains individually to discuss your needs.
• Ski Esprit: Three- to four-day programs. Explore both mountains with an instructor guide. Video analysis, race training and fun races, on-mountain brunch, lift priority on most lifts, awards and après activities are all part of the package. Ski programs start Fridays and Mondays.

Ticket options

Choices, choices. How much you pay for your downhill ski time is a matter of research into a blizzard of options, including day passes, multiday passes, seasons tickets, off-peak-season specials, accommodation/ski packages, and more.

Dual-mountain ski passes, trail maps, and information about rental equipment are available at the Activity and Information Centre. Both single- and dual-mountain tickets, for single and multiple days, are available at each mountain. Ticket categories are Seniors (65 and over), Adults (19 and over), Youth (13–18), Child (7–12). Tots (6 and under) ski free.

Both Blackcomb and Whistler mountains offer discount cards. Blackcomb's is called the Express Card. With it, you get your first day free and discounted lift tickets and ski services. Whistler Mountain's Ski Card also features discounts on lift tickets, a free first day, and discounts on

ski services and food specials. Both passes can be used as a credit card. On your first run of the day, your pass is electronically scanned by lift-line attendants and your ticket charged directly to your real credit card.

To save money, remember that during Regular Season, rates are highest; Value Season rates are lower. Dates for each mountain vary, so check to see what suits you best. The busiest time of the year, and the most expensive, is the Christmas holiday season, including New Year's Day. Late spring skiing discounts, from April to the end of May,

can offer considerable savings.

Pre-season ticket prices are discounted, both for lifts and ski lessons. If you buy early enough, you can reap significant savings. During the ski season, discounts on lift tickets are often available in Vancouver supermarkets.

Group rates (for 25 or more) include discount ski tickets. Group activities include dual slalom races, barbecues, brunches, videotaping, awards and après-ski functions. Corporate meetings, seminars, sports club get-togethers, and association events can be arranged to include ski activities.

Skier's responsibility code

THE MOUNTAINS are tough on skiers who don't obey the rules of safety. People found skiing within permanently closed or avalanche-closed areas will lose their skiing privileges (and may lose their lives). In addition, anyone requiring rescue or assistance found outside designated runs or ski area boundary, or within permanently closed or avalanche areas, is held

responsible for the cost of the rescue. Other rules of conduct include the following:

1. Ski under control and in a manner such that you can stop and avoid other skiers and objects.

2. When skiing downhill or overtaking another skier, you must avoid the skier below you.

3. Do not stop where you obstruct a trail or are not

visible from above.

4. When entering a trail or starting downhill, yield to other skiers.

5. All skiers shall wear retention straps or other devices to prevent runaway skis or snowboards.

6. Keep off closed trails and posted areas; ski within area boundaries.

Breathtaking views are part of the Whistler/Blackcomb skiing experience

The Whistler/Blackcomb ski area is consistently rated as one of the best in the world

Race programs

Racing is a highlight of the Whistler winter season. Competitive ski events include the World Cup/Whistler Mountain Ski Classic and Blackcomb's Kokanee Challenge Race Series and World Cup Freestyle. Other race events are designed for amateur ski competitors, including men, women, and snowboarders. The CIBC Canadian Disabled Championships features races on both mountains for disabled skiers.

A brief history of speed

World Cup skiers travel all over the world, defying gravity at 130 kilometres per hour. Few televised sports events offer the excitement and thrills of the World Cup.

International World Cup downhill racing returned to Whistler in 1993, with commitments to keep coming back to 1997. In March, skiers compete in back-to-back weekends in the Men's World Cup

Racing events are featured from January to May

Downhill and Super G. The course is the 3803-metre Dave Murray downhill, named for one of Canada's famous "Crazy Canuck" national ski team racers.

Races are accompanied by special events and partying, earning the World Cup circuit the nickname the White

Carnival.

Variations on a theme

The Inuit, Canada's northern aboriginal people, have more than a dozen words for snow. In and around Whistler, there are almost as many ways to enjoy it. Although Whistler's

---

What to watch for and where to watch

THE KITZBÜHEL WORLD Cup downhill has its Steilhang, or steep hill. Wengen has the narrow Hunschaff, and Val Gardena has its Camel Bumps. At Whistler, there's the Funnel and the Weasel.

Leaving the hut

A sharp incline is followed by three quick bumps. Racing at 100 kilometres per hour, skiers hit the Funnel, a steep, narrow pitch, followed by a demanding left-hand turn onto the Weasel.

The Weasel

The steepest and wildest pitch of the Whistler Mountain Ski Classic. Racers hang on for dear life, making the Weasel the most exciting viewpoint on the course.

It's easy to reach, just below Raven's Nest Café on Expressway.

Afterburner

At 120 kilometres per hour, skiers negotiate a fast fallaway turn onto Afterburner and a tight right-hand turn at Coach's Corner. There are some great vantage points in this area, but it's tricky to reach them. Watch for signs and be prepared to do a little hiking.

Hot Air

Two turns precede Hot Air, a new jump that is one of the biggest on the entire World Cup Circuit. Although it's easier to get there on skis (from Lower Franz's), it's possible to walk up the course to this popular viewpoint.

The finish line

The first thing you see when you get to Whistler Creek is a barrage of international media, personalities, and excitement. A natural amphitheatre and a huge television screen make this the most comfortable place to watch. Watch the racers' reactions to their performances and track the results.

Tip: Before any race, it's a good idea to scout the entire length of the course on one of the training days, then return to your favourite spots on race day.

For complete race listings, contact each mountain.

two major mountains are undeniably the main attraction, sports like heli-skiing can take you further afield to snow-covered glaciers high above the crowds. Others prefer Whistler's 22 kilometres of cross-country ski trails or hopping on board a snowmobile for backcountry exploring. For purists, there's snowshoeing, with barely a sound to break the silence of pristine wilderness. Snowboarding, back-country touring, sleigh rides, and bus-snow tours round out the possibilities.

Many tours can be booked by calling the Whistler Activity and Information Centre. Or you can book directly with the outfitters listed in this section.

Snowboarding

Vastly popular with skiers of all ages, snowboarding appeared on Whistler Resort slopes some 10 years ago. Recently *Snowboard Canada* magazine rated Whistler/Blackcomb the number-one snowboarding venue in the world. Both mountains are open to snowboarders and have half-pipes.

Skiers share the mountains with snowboarders in a sometimes uneasy truce. To encourage harmony, Whistler consulted with resorts south of

Steve Podborski

DON'T EXPECT TO catch Steve Podborski in his Whistler office. A man with a mission, he's in perpetual motion around the resort. The former downhill champion has discovered new passions, including snowboarding, mountain biking, golf, and in-line skating. "When I moved here, I knew intellectually this was a fabulous place to come to do all kinds of things, not just skiing. Now that I've scratched the surface, I can only say, Wow! This is a complex and rich place."

Steve has lived a life that's the dream of all athletes. Born in Don Mills, Ontario, in 1957, he grew up skiing on the slopes of Southern Ontario and racing in the local programs. In 1973, at the age of 16, he was named to the National Alpine Ski Team to race in the Can-Am Series.

In his first race on that tour in Whistler, Steve brought home a Silver Medal. The following year, 1974, he was promoted to the World Cup Tour. After winning a Bronze Medal in the 1980 Lake Placid Olympic Games (first downhill medal for a North American), he became the first non-European to win the World Cup downhill title in 1982.

Steve Podborski

During his career, Steve was ranked number one in the world for over two years and won eight individual World Cup competitions, including twice in a row on the most notorious and treacherous downhill race of all, the Hahnenkahm in Kitzbühel, Austria.

After 11 years on the Canadian Alpine Team as the most decorated downhill ski racer in North America, Steve retired in 1984 at the age of 26. During his career, he'd established a virtually unmatched record of 46 top 10 finishes out of 89 races. Add to that the eight individual World Cup victories, leaving him ranked fifth in the world all-time in the com-

pany of Austria's Franz Klammer and Switzerland's Pete Mueller. Many honours include Canada's Athlete of the Year twice and Ontario Athlete of the Year twice. Steve was named an Officer of the Order of Canada in 1982 and was inducted into the Canada Sports Hall of Fame in 1987 and the Honour Roll of the Canadian Ski Museum in 1988.

Since retiring, Steve has made his niche in Whistler with his wife, Kathy, and their children, Benjamin and Madelaine. He's director of corporate programs for Blackcomb Mountain, host of an hour-long morning television show, *Today on Blackcomb with Steve Podborski,* and host of a winter weekly television show, *Ski Base,* on TSN.

Somehow he still finds time for sports, including racing in *Legends* events broadcast by CBS Sports throughout the winter. "Whistler is so multi-dimensional," he says. "If you want golf, you have it. Or if you're a wild-eyed athlete with fire in your eyes, you can go for the outrageously good mountain biking or tough backcountry touring. You don't have to be pigeonholed."

Paragliding provides the ultimate high

the border, formed a snowboard task force, and boosted its awareness campaign. Stricter rules were put into effect regarding conduct.

Now both mountains welcome snowboarders throughout the season with daily and multiday programs for adults and children. Private lessons are available. Whistler Mountain's weekend Oxygen Adult Snowboard Camp suits all levels of riders. Blackcomb Mountain teaches basics of balance, control, and turning, as well as offering a technique tune-up and carving clinic for experienced boarders. For youth programs, 12–16 years, see, "Whistler for Kids."

Most downhill rental shops offer snowboard rentals. In addition, contact the following:
• Showcase Snowboards: 938-2018
• Snoboard Shop: 932-4440
• Attitude at Altitude: 932-8981

Cross-country skiing

The Lost Lake Cross Country Trail system winds through 22 kilometres of diverse and scenic terrain, starting from the trailhead adjacent to the Whistler Village day ski parking lot off Lorimer Road.

All beginner, intermediate, and advanced trails are groomed and track set for ski skating and touring techniques. A cosy hut perched on the shore of Lost Lake and the clubhouse at the Chateau Whistler golf course provide rest stops along the way.

Delightfully, 4 kilometres of trails are lit from 4:00 pm to 11:00 pm for night skiing.

Additional cross-country track-set trails around the Whistler Golf Course are an ideal beginner's route. Another popular trip is to the Ancient Cedars, north of Emerald Estates between Whistler and Pemberton in the Sixteen Mile Creek/Cougar Mountain area. This 50-kilometre route circles 1000-year-old trees and is shared by snowmobilers and cross-country ski enthusiasts.

A cross-country day ticket or pass must be purchased to ski the Lost Lake trails. Call the Lost Lake Ticket Booth at 932-6436. Passes may be purchased at the Myrtle Philip Community Centre: 932-3113.

Trail maps and information about rental equipment are available at the Whistler Activity and Information Centre, or by calling one of the following companies:
• Blackcomb Ski & Sport: 938-7749
• Whistler Mountain Sport Shop: 932-5422/932-6712
• Sports West: 938-7777
• Village Sport Stop: 932-5495

Heli-skiing

Heli-skiing is the perfect winter/spring activity for intermediate and advanced skiers. Ski the area's numerous glaciers above the clouds, from 2438 to 4877 vertical metres. The following outfitters offer a range of three- to six-run packages, private group tours, heli-ski weeks, gourmet lunches, and transportation.
• Mountain Heli-Sports: 932-2070/1-800-661-6302
• Tyax Heli-Skiing Ltd.: 932-7007; Fax: 932-2500
• Tyax Lodge Heli-skiing (Gold Bridge): 1-800-667-4854
• Western Canadian Heli-Sports: 938-1700
• Whistler Heli-Skiing: 932-4105; Fax: 938-1225
• Coast Glacier Skiing (Squamish): 898-9016

Snowmobiling

Snowmobiles take visitors off the beaten track to scenic backcountry areas, working ranches, old-growth forests and to the heights of local mountains. There's nothing like an 1828-metre vantage point for a superior view of the Coast Mountains, or a journey across the vast Pemberton Ice Fields. A popular destination is the Ancient Cedars, a grove of 1000-year-old trees north of Whistler. Another option is a sunset or full-moon tour atop Blackcomb Mountain, complete with fine dining.

Snowmobiles are quieter, smoother, and cleaner these days, and drivers are more environmentally sensitive. Tours are for beginner to advanced levels and include certified guides, snowsuits, helmets, warm boots, gourmet meals, and transportation to and from Whistler Village. Reservations are sometimes required. Contact the following companies for full details of available tours:

- The Canadian Snowmobile Adventure Company (Blackcomb Mountain tours): 938-1616; Fax: 938-1618
- Blackcomb Snowmobiling: 932-8484; Fax: 932-8410
- McLeod Creek Wilderness Ranch (Pemberton): 894-5704
- Whistler Snowmobile/ Whistler Backcountry Adventures (Ancient Cedars/Pemberton Ice Fields): 932-4086

Whistler and Blackcomb mountains welcome safety-conscious snowboarders

Snowboard rider's code

OUT-OF-CONTROL snowboarders are not welcome on the mountains. Respect the following rules:

1. Always ride under control and in such a way that you can stop or avoid obstacles.

2. When passing a person on the hill, you must yield the right of way. Avoid the person and do not disrupt his or her course.

3. Do not stop where you obstruct a trail or are not visible to oncoming traffic. When you do stop, be sure it's at the side of the hill where oncoming traffic can see you at a distance. When stopped, face uphill so that you can avoid those skiers, just in case they can't avoid you.

4. When entering a trail or starting downhill, yield to all others. Let them go by; then, if you want, go by them.

5. Snowboarders must wear a leash to prevent a runaway board. Your leash can double as a shoulder strap or as a lock.

6. Keep off closed trails and out-of-bounds areas and observe posted signs. Avoid the temptation to ride backcountry or closed trails. If you're lucky, you'll only lose your lift ticket. Why risk damaging your equipment or injuring yourself? Ride smart, safely, and without worry.

7. Unhitch your back foot when getting on the lift. Nothing looks more pathetic than a snowboarder dragging along a snow fence like a lame animal.

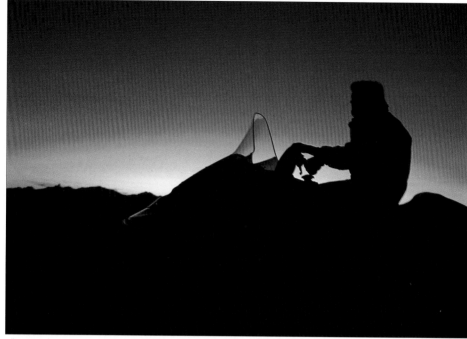

Snowmobiling gives access to the backcountry to non-skiers

Snowshoeing

You can't get a more Canadian experience than snowshoeing. Native people used snowshoes for transportation and recreation before European settlement in North America. Embraced by fur trappers, snowshoes later inspired special clubs, the first established in Montreal in 1843 by prominent local businessmen. Competitive racing was introduced in the 1860s, but a fad for skating and a new winter sport, ice hockey, in the 1890s ended snowshoeing's popularity. At Whistler, morning, afternoon, and evening deluxe tours are offered for ages 6 to 65+. Guided 90-minute treks along forest trails begin with rentals and instruction. Longer trips to a local glacial lake, including lunch, are available.

• Canadian Snowshoe Services: 938-3003/932-2394

Sleigh rides

Whether a fun-filled sleigh ride for the whole group or an old-fashioned horse and carriage ride for two, excursions for up to 14 people tour the Whistler and Pemberton areas. Evenings often include bonfires and sing-alongs.

• Whistler Outdoor Experience Company: 932-3389

• McLeod Creek Wilderness Ranch: 894-5704/894-6944
• Layton Bryson Outfitting and Trail Riding: 932-6623
• Western Adventures on Horseback: 894-6155/ 894-6968

Snow-country sightseeing

If you prefer to admire snow

The 10 best questions

ACCORDING TO LOCALS, the following are the 10 "best" questions asked by tourists while in Whistler:

10. Where do you live?
9. Can I get my change in American?
8. What happens to the snow when it rains?
7. Do you live here?
6. Is it always cloudy when it snows?
5. Are these prices in American?
4. What time is it on top of the mountain?
3. Can we drink the water here?
2. Where are the dog sleds and igloos?
1. What do you do with the moguls in the summer?

from a distance, a Super Snow Bus excursion or glacier air tour is the answer.

Backcountry-bound on old logging roads, a fully enclosed, heated all-terrain vehicle takes you along the banks of the Lillooet River to Meager Creek Hot Springs. You break new trails through deep powder snow to arrive at the snow-shrouded hot springs north of Pemberton.

Glacier air tours are another alternative. Fly high over the Squamish area, known as the Valley of 1000 Glaciers. If you choose, you can land and take a short walk on these ancient snowfields. Remember not to lean on the plane, or you may have to walk back.

- McLeod Creek Wilderness Ranch (Pemberton): 894-5704
- Glacier Air Tours: 898-9016, (Squamish), 932-2705 (Whistler), 683-0209 (Vancouver)

Weatherview

On the mountains, you can actually experience three seasons in one day: wet at lower elevations, snowing at midstation, and sunny at the top. Dress in layers, with a waterproof outer layer. An extra pair of gloves and a cloth for wiping your goggles are also recommended by the experts.

Average alpine temperature
- December-February: Low -12°C, high -5°C
- March-May: Low -8°C, high 5°C

Check it out

BEFORE SETTING OUT, call the Environment Canada Weather Report: 932-5413.

Cross-country skiing is still the first choice of many

Backcountry touring

A FEW MINUTES on Highway 99 and it's obvious just how vast BC's mountains are. And behind the slopes you see are others waiting to be discovered.

Accessible by snowmobile and heli-ski companies in winter, the backcountry's glaciers and crystal snows serve up a truly impressive landscape. A series of icefields begins here and extends 400 kilometres northwest, creating one of the largest areas of ice in the temperate regions of the world.

The Pemberton Ice Fields (also called Pemberton Ice Cap) adds up to over 240 square kilometres of undulating, ridable terrain north of Whistler. At 2134 metres above sea level, the snow-bound vistas are vast and primordial. Since this is one of the smaller icefields in the area, tours here are relatively safe, with few crevasse problems. Beginners as well as experienced snowmobilers will enjoy this trip.

When the weather permits, the party continues outdoors

Warming up après-ski

Partying after a day of skiing is a time-honoured tradition, starting with après and ending when the clubs, lounges, and bars close. Whistler is no exception: the action starts in the late afternoon, often with live entertainment, and continues to closing in the early morning hours.

Village Square, at the base of both mountains, is the main draw after a day on the slopes. Weather permitting, patios at Chez Joël and Citta are open, with the Longhorn Saloon (Carleton Lodge), Twigs (next to Delta Mountain Inn), and Brandy's at the Keg nearby.

After 8:00 pm, try a dance circuit of the Savage Beagle, Tommy Africa's, and Garfinkel's (below Chez Joël).

Each has its own particular ambience. There's rock 'n' roll at Garfinkel's and a taped dance mix at the Savage Beagle. Tommy Africa's dance floor is big, with a swirling light system to set the mood.

- Locals hang out at the Boot Pub, north of Whistler Village in the Shoestring Lodge, Tapley's in the Village, and Hoz's on Lake Placid Drive at Whistler Creek. The Boot Pub, just off Highway 99, is the oldest bar in the area. Bands play nightly, and the

Don't drink and drive

THE SEA TO SKY Highway on a winter's night is not an easy drive. Needless to say, you need your full faculties to make it down to Vancouver unscathed. Above all else, don't drink and drive.

atmosphere is comfortable and low-key. Tapley's offers a full pub menu and selection of domestic beers. Hoz's is laid back, with TV sports and darts. Sports fans will also enjoy Jimmy D's at the Fairway Hotel, with its giant TV screen, darts, and pool table.

- Live entertainment is also presented nightly at Buffalo Bill's, from country and western to rock. The Border Cantina, upstairs from the Boot Pub, serves Mexican food and occasional live music.

In and around Chateau Whistler at Blackcomb Benchlands, afternoons start early in the land of the M Bars: Monk's, Merlins, and the Mallard Bar. The last, located on the main floor of the Chateau Whistler, and Crystal's Lounge, a piano bar in the

Crystal Lodge in Whistler Village, are both ideal for intimate evenings.

Best for romance

For some, the mountains are a mere backdrop. If your prime purpose in visiting Whistler Resort is a romantic interlude, you won't be disappointed.

In the early days, pioneer Alex Philip rowed young lovers across Alta Lake on moonlit nights to kindle romance. As the author of three romantic novels, one of which was made into a movie, he used the impressive vistas of the area as backdrop. At Rainbow Park, the site of the Philip's famous Rainbow Lodge, you can still cross Alex's Bridge of Sighs, albeit a replica of the original. For decades, newlyweds flocked to Rainbow Lodge, then came back to celebrate anniversaries.

Whistler continues to be famous for romance. Locals marry here, as do Japanese visitors. Weddings take place on mountaintops, in hotels, near secluded lakes, in chapels—anywhere imagination can take a bride and groom. Couples from Japan marry through an interpreter, who manages everything from the bride's coiffeur and the groom's tuxedo to their wedding vows.

Whistler nightlife

Lounges, bars, and clubs
- Araxi's Antipasto Bar: 932-4540. Whistler Village. Daily; 11:00 am to 1:00 am.
- Black's Pub: 932-6945. Above the Original Ristorante, Whistler Village. English-style fare. Patio.
- Brandy's Lounge: 932-5151. Adjacent to the Keg, Whistler Village.
- Briar's Lounge: 932-2522. Whistler Fairways Hotel, Whistler Village.
- Buffalo Bill's: 932-5211. Timberline Lodge, Whistler Village. Live entertainment to 2:00 am.
- Chez Joël Lounge: 932-2112. 4232 Village Stroll.
- Cinnamon Bear Bar: 932-1982. Delta Mountain Inn, Whistler Village. Sports bar.
- Citta: 932-4177. 4232 Village Stroll.
- Garfinkel's: 932-2323. Downstairs at Skiers Approach, Whistler Village. Classic rock. Dance floor.
- Il Caminetto di Umberto: 932-4442.
- Jimmy D's Sports Bar: 932-4451. Whistler Fairways Hotel, Whistler Village. Sports bar. Patio.
- Longhorn Saloon & Grill:

Live entertainers

932-5999. Carleton Lodge, Whistler Village. Patio.
- Crystal's Lounge: 932-2221. Crystal Lodge, Whistler Village. Live entertainment on weekends. Snacks served.
- O'Doul's Sports Bar: 932-3433 or 932-1133, in the Listel Hotel, 4121 Village Green.
- Savage Beagle Club: 932-4540. Whistler Village. Dancing until 2:00 am.
- Tapley's Neighbourhood Pub: 932-4022. Across from Whistler Conference Centre, Whistler Village. Patio.
- Tommy Africa's: 932-6090.

Downstairs at Gateway Drive, Whistler Village. Dance floor. Open to 2:00 am.
- Trattoria di Umberto Lounge: 932-5858.
- Twigs: 932-1982, ext. 229. Next to Delta Mountain Inn.
- The Mallard Bar: 938-2430. Chateau Whistler. Piano, live entertainment. Patio.
- Merlin's: 932-3141. Daylodge, base of Blackcomb. Patio.
- Monk's Grill: 932-9677. Blackcomb Benchlands.
- Phil's Lounge: 932-9795. Le Chamois. Occasional live entertainment.

Beyond central
- The Boot Pub: 932-4246. Shoestring Lodge, 1 kilometre north of Whistler Village. Live entertainment.
- Border Cantina: 932-3373. Upstairs at Shoestring Lodge.
- Dusty's Den: 932-3434. Base of Whistler Mountain, Whistler Creek. Patio.
- Hoz's Pub: 932-5940. Whistler Resort & Club, Lake Placid Road, Whistler Creek. Daily; pub fare to 11:00 pm.
- Rim Rock Café & Oyster Bar: 932-5565. Whistler Creek.

A relaxing evening by the fire is always sociable

Romance also begins here: in lounges, on hiking trails, standing in line to board a lift. Strangers become friends… and in more than one case, a chance meeting has led to marriage.

Here are suggestions for the best of togetherness.

Chocolate is heavenly

February is the month for love, and in Whistler, it's also the month for chocolates. Beginning in early February, chocolate creations are prepared by the resort's best chefs. A chocolate-lover's tour includes six sample desserts. Call 932-2394 for complete details.

Sunset dining

The top-of-the-mountain view at Blackcomb's Christine's, at 1200 metres, has won this restaurant kudos as one of the

Whistler is sweet enough for any traveller

Honeymooners holidaying at Rainbow Lodge

Pacific Northwest's most romantic dining spots. Open seven days a week during the ski season, the restaurant affords a 360-degree panoramic view of mountains and sky.

During the summer months, sunset dining (at 6:00 pm and 8:00 pm on Saturday) at Christine's begins in early July and continues for a limited number of evenings to early September. Sunday brunches (from 11:30 am to 2:30 pm) begin at the same time. Oozing with romance, Christine's offers a fixed-price sunset gourmet menu with multiple choices, poetically described on the menu—for example, carpaccio (rare lamb tenderloin served with asiago and rosemary–infused olive oil) and warm roast garlic bulb (with warmed brie, pecans, and herb bread) just for

starters. Desserts may include Grand Marnier pecan pie, white and dark chocolate mile-high mousse cake, and crème caramel with fresh berries. Reservations recommended. Call 938-7437 (ski season and weekends) or 938-7353 (summer weekdays).

Moonlight dine and ski

Four times a year, Whistler Mountain presents an evening of fine dining, followed by skiing in the moonlight. If you're a skier in love, this is just the ticket. For complete details, call 932-3434.

Numbers game

THINKING OF APPLYING for a job with Whistler Mountain?

- Number of applications received (August-November 1993) by the Human Resources Department: 3000
- Where they were from: Australia, Japan, and Ontario/Eastern provinces
- How many were interviewed: 1400
- How many were hired: 300 new staff

- Look who's back: 322 returning staff
- How many never leave: 81 year-round staff
- Anyone else? 281 volunteers (every one of them gets interviewed as well)
- Total staff count: 984
- Total number of turkey dinners served at annual staff Christmas party: 1000 (with spouses and children)

Sleep in peace

A real log chalet with all the amenities is a must for romantic couples. Local companies know how to lay on the luxuries.

Take Brew Creek Lodge, for example, 15 minutes south of Whistler. Enter the lodge via a secluded 1-kilometre road. Each building on the grounds is handcrafted, constructed almost entirely out of timber with vaulted post-and-beam ceilings, custom wood bed frames, and stone fireplaces, which is probably why so many workshops are booked in here. There's a whirlpool, dry sauna, and heli-pad for quick getaways to Powder Mountain, five minutes away and 3658 vertical metres away—by helicopter.

Log chalets can be booked through one of Whistler's accommodation rental companies. For Brew Creek Lodge, call direct at 932-7210 or toll-free from Vancouver at 682-7221; Fax: 932-7223.

Festival of Lights

SOMETHING ABOUT A snow-swathed valley sparkling with Christmas lights adds to winter's excitement. Before the busy US Thanksgiving weekend, Whistler's Festival of Lights begins to garland the valley. The festival has four categories: restaurant and hotel, retail and office, residential, and multi-family residence. As many as 800 multicoloured lights decorate some residences. Noteworthy displays: Chateau Whistler, Re/Max of Whistler.

Things locals like to do

- Sunbathing nude at Lucille Lake.
- Skiing the trees and cliffs off Blackcomb's Fraggle Rock
- Hiking up to Phalanx Ridge and skiing down
- Skiing to the top of Blackcomb Glacier, then looking over the other side—"The total silence that's there is awesome."
- Soaking in the Meager Creek Hot Springs
- Hanging out at the Boot Pub
- Riding really tough mountain bike trails – "Single-track mountain biking where tourists wouldn't go—logs, rocks, roots."
- Shopping at farmers' markets in Pemberton and Mount Currie
- Great coffee north of Whistler at Pemberton's the Pony Expresso or Mount Currie's Spirit Circle Art, Craft & Tea Company
- Spotting bears chilling out on the mountains in spring
- Canoeing on Lillooet Lake—"on a moonlit night"
- Volunteering time as an on-mountain host in return for ski passes

Dave Muller, Whistler Mountain groomer

A NIGHT IN THE LIFE. It's a long, lonely night on Whistler Mountain for its 36 groomers. Veteran driver Dave Muller has worked for the mountain for 10 seasons. Take a peek inside his diary of a typical night shift.

11:15 pm Arrive at locker room. Pull on my mountain uniform and strap on radio. Head up the mountain, by snowmobile or cat.

12:05 am Travelling to the first run, testing the snow for conditions to decide on the proper implement to be used for the night: a tiller for moist conditions, compactor bar for fresh snow, or powder maker for hard, compacted snow. Tonight the snow is wet, so I've got the tiller on.

12:30 am Arrive at my first run, Upper Franz's...you have to hang a quarter of your driver's side track over the edge of the run to capture the snow that has been pushed into a berm along the bank. It's a long way down from this edge to the trees. Every once in a while, I slip a little and have to pull my blade up to get control of the cat again.

3:30 am It took me three hours to groom Franz's, along with the in-run from Upper Whiskey Jack and out-run to midstation. Just enough time left for one

Dave Muller's midnight grooming ensures smooth slopes

more quick run before lunch. Fisheye is next.

5:00 am Lunchtime. Sandwiches and coffee are welcome now, because the most fatiguing part of the shift, when it starts to get light, is coming soon. But first I call the snow phone reporter to give her the weather conditions.

6:30 am More grooming. This time, it's Highway 86 to the peak. I make two up and one down pass from the bottom of Upper Franz's through Grand Finale to Frog Hollow, then head for the peak on the inside pass.

Getting to the top of the

Khyber is fairly straightforward, as the wind causes little drifting in this section. Several back-ups at the Khyber entrance, and I'm off and up toward Cockalorum. From here, the drifting gets worse as we get higher. Sometimes it's almost impossible to even find this road. Then finish off the peak road to Symphony Bowl, pushing large drifts off the Glacier Cirque and Saddle.

The sun is rising now. What a place to be for sunrise. Nothing compares. I have the best job anywhere.

Mayor Ted Nebbeling

THE SECOND BEST job in town (after Dave Muller's) belongs to Whistler Mayor Ted Nebbeling, now in his second term. The mayor gets to ski with royalty and international celebrities, and it's practically part of the job description.

A hotel manager by training,

Dutch-born Nebbeling moved to Whistler in 1980. Go-getter that he is, he once ran a total of nine businesses, including a gourmet deli and five clothing stores. But life isn't all fun and games; the mayor is faced with issues that include development sprawl, affordable housing, and communi-

ty spirit.

If you think Whistler service is tops, it may be because of the Whistler Spirit Course. Offered by the Whistler Resort Association with Nebbeling's enthusiastic support, it educates residents and employees about the resort and how to respond to tourists.

Whistler's new Meadow Park Sports Centre reflects area growth

Way to grow

An estimated 20,000 people live along the Sea to Sky Highway between the boundary of the Greater Vancouver Regional District and the Resort Municipality of Whistler. Beyond Whistler, the regional district's population is only 5500, the majority in Lillooet.

Squamish is home to 12,000 residents, and Whistler's share of the total is some 5000 year-round residents. During peak tourism periods, as many as 26,000 visitors swell the resort.

As you drive Highway 99 from Horseshoe Bay to Whistler, signs of growth are evident. In Lions Bay, population 1330, few lots remain. Furry Creek includes a golf course as well as 1000 residential lots. Britannia Beach, because of its mining history and leftover pollutants, poses a cleanup problem and may be bypassed. Porteau Bluffs could eventually see development on waterfront land.

Squamish, which controls much of the land in the Sea to Sky corridor, is feeling the pressure. Although steep topography, extensive Crown forest land, hazardous areas and Garibaldi Provincial Park stand in the way, sizable bench lands may be developed.

Whistler itself is seeing tremendous growth. By the year 2002, planners predict numbers could double along Highway 99, with Whistler's year-round population climbing to 12,000 and its recreational population to 42,000. The fact that secured parking spaces, "ideal for retailers, office workers, home builders and home owners," were being sold in spring 1994 in Whistler Village Centre for $18,900 each is an indication of how far the resort has come since its early ski days. Of course the parking space comes with a free daily car wash.

Big plans are in store for Whistler, many of which are already under way. Blackcomb Benchlands is growing, with a new subdivision going in, as well as hotels, condominiums, and retail outlets. Whistler North, a 15-year-project adjacent to Whistler Village, is well under way. The town will have a host of new hotels, a third golf course, a 16-court tennis resort, and a 160-kilometre world-renowned mountain bike route that is sure to attract international visitors.

To counteract the explosion of development, town planners are trying to enhance amenities and services for year-round residents. The Myrtle Philip Community Centre and Meadow Park Arena opened for residents and visitors in 1992. A medical clinic,

Olympic-size swimming pool, and new library are in the works. Another goal is to diversify the economy, with more balance between recreation and industry. Overall, say planners, growth management will remain a fact of life in the Whistler community.

Location, location, location

For developers, the conclusion in the Whistler area is definitely, "build it and they will come." For many visitors, it's buy and buy now.

A variety of options is available, from converted hotel rooms transformed into efficiency apartments in the range

Million-dollar views inspire million-dollar chalets

of 200 square feet to one- and two-bedroom condominiums, brand new homes and established properties, time-share purchases, and resort club

ownership.

Realtors point out that the cost per square foot of recreational condominiums on Blackcomb Benchlands is

Other winter activities

CONSIDERING THAT WINTER was once the off-season for the Whistler area, the amount of activity now available is almost overwhelming. Both Blackcomb and Whistler mountains organize a continuous series of events to enhance their weekly activities. Community efforts, natural phenomena, and entrepreneurial zeal also add to the mix.

The Festivals and Events Calendar, updated annually, is distributed by the Whistler Resort Association. Winter officially kicks off with opening day in late November, with December events hard on its heels.

The Christmas season is big time. The Bizarre Bazaar!, an annual Christmas craft show at Myrtle Philip Community School presented by the Whistler Arts Council (932-2129), comes early in the month. Like many events, there's no charge to drop in and check out local arts and crafts, in-

cluding pottery, jewellery, wood carving, and weaving. Whistler Resort Ski Club Week, in mid-December, means ski clubs can take advantage of values during a week of skiing and racing. For the children, there's breakfast with Santa on Whistler Mountain and at Merlin's on Blackcomb Mountain. Just after Christmas, enjoy free concerts at Chateau Whistler, with Renaissance and romantic tunes (932-8310; Fax: 932-4461). A moonlight dine and ski on Whistler Mountain with candlelight dinner at Pika's restaurant is held every month, December through March.

January through May, activities continue apace. For more special days, see the SuperGuide Calendar on page 95. For an updated version of the annual *Whistler Resort Festivals and Events* calendar, contact the Whistler Activity and Information Centre at 932-2394.

The new Myrtle Philip Community Centre, located on Lorimer Road in Whistler Cay, offers residents and visitors aerobics classes, drop-in volleyball, basketball, badminton, cross-country day tickets, and a cross-country full-moon ski-and-dine package. Over the holidays, try one-day courses such as Christmas wreath making or creative centrepiece arrangements.

Also new, the Meadow Park Arena, 6 kilometres north of Whistler Village on Highway 99, is an NHL-sized ice surface with a 350-seat spectator section. Skating and hockey programs and public skating are offered seven days a week. Skate rentals and sharpening are available during public skating hours. Contact the Myrtle Philip Community Centre and Meadow Park Sports Centre at 938-7275.

lower than that found at eight other world-renowned ski destinations.

Not only are the prices lower (if you have the money in the first place), but in many cases, you get something unavailable at most world-class resorts: ski-in and ski-out capability from your front door.

For comparison shoppers, Japan's Yuzawa resort is the most expensive in the world at more than CDN$560 per square foot. At Courchevel in France and at Aspen in Colorado, recreational accommodation is about $400 per square foot. Vail is a slightly less at $330 to $400. The Italian resorts at Courmayer and Cervina are valued at $300, and condos at Australia's Mount Buller are priced in the $240 to $270 range. Blackcomb condominiums sell at about $200 per square foot.

Another approach is timeshare ownership. In return for attending a 90-minute sales presentation by a vacation ownership company, potential clients receive gifts or dining certificates. Owners buy a week or two of resort time, for a fee anywhere from $7000 to $15,000. Resort club membership, introduced by Intrawest, owners of Blackcomb Mountain, works in a similar way.

Icy adventures

Although it is not attracting hoards as yet, ice climbing is growing in popularity in the Whistler area. One of the toughest sports, requiring both physical and mental strength, ice climbing has a number of locales. Most spectacular is Shannon Falls's, a 45-minute drive south of Whistler in

A bergschrund in the Pemberton Ice Cap

Shannon Falls Provincial Park. Watching a climber pick away at Shannon Falls' 300-metre vertical slope is awe-inspiring. (Check with BC Parks before you attempt this yourself.) Other routes include the bluffs of the Soo River just north of Whistler, the Green River, and Blackcomb Mountain. Climbers also tackle the Cayoosh Canyon and Bridge River Canyon on Highway 99 enroute to Lillooet.

Ice climbing courses are offered by Escape Route Mountain Specialists (938-3338/ 938-3228) and Pacific High

Mountain Guides in Squamish (892-5859/892-9662).

An easier way to experience winter's icy majesty is to visit one of two underground caves. The first, a snow cave on the lower part of Whistler Bowl near the Peak Chair, opened in spring 1992. A skier dropped into it, then walked out of the 46-metre-deep by 91-metre-long cave unscathed. Not to be outdone, nature opened an ice cave on the Horstman Glacier at Blackcomb over the summer.

Known by mountaineers as bergschrund, underground ice

Ice climbing at Shannon Falls

caves are part of a giant crevasse traversing a glacier. Studies into the future of bergschrund in the area are ongoing. Because a cave's shape and size can change within a few weeks, mountain specialists collect extensive data, including air and snow temperatures, to predict their stability. A permanent interpretive centre may be established, based on a program now operating at the Columbia Icefields near Jasper.

For more information on bergschrund, contact Blackcomb Mountain. In the summer, Blackcomb offers free guided tours into the Horstman Glacier ice cave.

Heli-skiing near Whistler

WHISTLER MOUNTAIN RENTALS

Rentals are available from both bases, Whistler Creekside and Whistler Village, at the following locations:

Whistler Creekside rentals

- Located by the Quicksilver Express chair, Whistler Creekside rentals offers a full selection of demo and high-performance skis and boots. Open midweek 8:30 am to 5:00 pm/weekends and holidays 8:00 am to 5:00 pm, 932-5422.

Whistler Village rentals

- Westbrook in Mountain Square (in front of Carleton Lodge): Salomon/Atomic/Rossignol Test Centre, where you can buy or rent from Salomon, Atomic, Rossignol, Lange, and Koflach. Midweek 8:30 am to 9:00 pm/ weekends and holidays 8:00 am to 9:00 pm, 932-2391.
- Village Gondola: On the doorstep of the Gondola, this shop sells skis and boots by Salomon. Midweek 8:30 am to 6:00 pm/weekends and holidays 8:00 am to 6:00 pm, 932-2311.
- Carleton Lodge: Downstairs in the Carleton Lodge in front of the Gondola. Spacious rental shop with boots, skis, and snowboards. Check your skis overnight and get an overnight wax/repair. Midweek 8:30 am to 6:00 pm/weekends and holidays 7:30 am-6:00 pm, 932-6712.

Ski school & demo/repair centre

- If you're at the top of Whistler Mountain and want to try the latest skis, you can field-test here. Equipment repair is also available. Phone 932-3434 and ask for the Alpine Demo Centre.

Cross-country ski races include amateurs and professionals

Blackcomb Mountain rentals

Several shops are located in the daylodge at the base of Blackcomb Mountain. Contact the following shops by calling 938-7749.

- Blackcomb Ski and Sport: Goggles, gloves, hats, and other accessories.
- Blackcomb Daylodge Rentals: Standard and children's, snowboards; clothing rentals.
- The High Performance Shop: Rental outlet for high-performance ski equipment.
- Showcase Snowboards: Retail, rental, and repair for snowboards; clothing, and accessories. Located in the Carleton Lodge.
- Blackcomb Ski Services: Edges sharpened and bevelled on the robotic Montana Stone Grinder.
- Kid's Only: Strictly for kids, retail and rental. Located in Kid's Kamp in the Blackcomb Administration Building.

Other rental shops

- Mile High Sports Rentals, 4599 Chateau Boulevard: 938-2012
- Spicy Sports, 4557 Blackcomb

Way: 938-1821
- Sports West, Two locations in Carleton Lodge: 938-7777
- Village Sport Stop, Whistler Village: 932-5495
- Whistler Bootfit, Delta Mountain Inn Hotel: 932-9669

Cross-country equipment rentals

Call the Whistler Activity and Information Centre: 932-2394 or the following companies:

- Mile High Sports: 938-7736
- Sports West, Carleton Lodge: 938-7777
- Village Sport Stop: 932-5495

Rental tips

- Avoid arriving at peak hours, between 9:00 am and 10:00 am.
- If possible, rent the night before.
- Have your identification ready.
- Before you get to the rental shop, jot down your particulars: height, weight, boot size, and skiing ability. You'll race through the rental form and be skiing faster.

Useful telephone numbers

- Emergency: 911
- Ambulance (non-emergency): 932-4233
- Fire (non-emergency): 932-2020; 932-5111
- Helpline for Children: Dial "O" and ask for Zenith 1234
- Kids' Help Line: 1-800-668-6868
- RCMP (non-emergency): 932-3440
- RCMP (emergency): 932-3044
- Poison Control: 1-800-667-3747
- Canadian Avalanche Rescue Dog Association: 932-1110
- Whistler Search and Rescue: 932-2328
- Highway Condition Information: 938-4997
- Municipal Hall (Resort Municipality of Whistler): 932-5535
- Whistler Activity and Information Centre: 932-2394

- Whistler Central Reservations: 932-4222
- Whistler Chamber of Commerce: 932-5528
- Whistler Conference Centre: 932-3928
- Whistler Museum and Archives Society: 932-2019
- Whistler Public Library: 932-5564
- Whistler Resort Association: 932-3928
- Vehicle Impound Yard: 8001 Highway 99

Public services
- Travel Infocentre, 2000 Lake Placid Road: 932-5528
- Whistler Transit System (bus): 932-4020. Ask for the free *Whistler Rider's Guide*, available in winter and summer editions
- BC Rail Station: 932-4003
- ICBC, at the Blackcomb Profes-

sional Building: 938-3137
- Day skier lot, Whistler Village: 938-1066
- Skiers Chapel, 2000 Lake Placid Road: 932-5528

Banks/cash machines
- Food Plus, Whistler Gateways, beside Boston Pizza: 932-6193
- North Shore Credit Union, 4321 Whistler Gate Boulevard: 932-5314; Fax: 932-8352
- Royal Bank of Canada: 101-4000 Whistler Way: 932-7079; Fax: 932-7073
- Toronto Dominion Bank Whistler's Marketplace: 932–9660

Taxi/chauffeur
- Sea to Sky Taxi: 938-3333 or 932-3333
- Town & Country Chauffeurs Inc.: 932-6468; Fax: 932-6448
- Whistler Taxi: 938-3333

Special days

THE FOLLOWING EVENTS are subject to change. To confirm, contact the Whistler Activity and Information Centre (932-2394).

Ongoing winter events
- Concerts in the Whistler Conference Centre
- Whistler Arts Council presentations (dance, cabaret, theatre)

November
- Opening Day of Ski Season (US Thanksgiving Weekend)

December
- Whistler Christmas Revue
- Breakfast with Santa
- Christmas at the Chateau
- Whistler Resort First Night New Year's Eve. Non-alcoholic outdoor celebrations

January
- Owens Corning World Freestyle Skiing Championships

Annual winter events include ice carving and wine tasting

- Whistler Chocolate Festival
- North American Police and Fire Games Ski Week

February
- Whistler Mountain Peak to Valley Race
- Gay Ski Week
- Bo of Snow Competition on Blackcomb. Triathlon event
- Chateau Whistler Cup Cross-

country event
- World Cup Downhill and Super G Races on Whistler Mountain

March
- Whistler Mountain Gallery's Annual World Cup Art Show
- Western Canadian Powder 8 Championships on Blackcomb
- CIBC Canadian Disabled Championships & Festivals

April
- Couloir Ski Race Extreme on Blackcomb Mountain
- International Masters' Championships on Whistler Mountain
- Whistler Cup International Juvenile Ski Race
- Parawest Paraglide Meet on Blackcomb Mountain
- Whistler Mountain winter ski season ends

Whistler in Summer

Live performances are the order of a summer's day

Whistler Resort is as much a summer destination as a winter one. Known for its cold-weather activities, the area has worked hard to make summer equally appealing. After only a few years of marketing and promotion, the number of visitors between May and the opening of the ski season in late November shows signs of rivalling that of the winter season.

This is good news for visitors, resulting in a real variety of organized activities. Or, if you prefer independent travel, Tourism British Columbia's Infocentres provide trail and backroads maps and local advice. Detailed recreation and nature guidebooks, covering everything from wildlife, trees, and plants to rock climbing, are also available from book-stores. See the SuperGuide reference section for suggestions.

Many organized summer activities can be booked through the Whistler Activity and Information Centre (932-2394) in Whistler Village: golf, tennis, horseback riding, whitewater rafting, kayaking, guided tours, heli-skiing, in-line skating, fishing, sailing, and more.

Cultural attractions can also be booked through the Whistler Activity and Information Centre. Throughout the summer, live theatre presentations, movies, street performances, art shows, workshops and seminars, popular band concerts, and symphony orchestra concerts take place.

Because Whistler has grown to make the most of its natural surroundings, many activities are free. Swim, sail, or windsurf at five lakes or picnic at six lakeside parks. Saunter or bike along the scenic, mostly paved, foot-friendly Valley Trail linking all of Whistler's parks.

A stroll through Whistler Village brings you to the chairlifts of both Whistler and Blackcomb mountains. Along with panoramic views, both mountains run a number of on-site eateries, as well as free guided tours once you're up top. Mountain biking is an option on both mountains.

On Blackcomb Mountain, try Horstman Glacier's unique summer skiing or snowboarding. The entire glacier is open for public skiing, from novice to experienced levels, noon to 3:00 pm, mid-June to early August, weather permitting. If you're feeling rusty, the Atomic Dave Murray Summer Ski Camps improve your recreational and/or racing techniques.

Don't neglect Whistler in late spring or fall. The resort is at its most uncrowded, hotel rates are lowest, and the weather is often dry and sunny. Many activities are operating; check ahead to plan your off-season time in Whistler.

Glacier gliding

From the top of the Musical Bumps and Singing Pass trails on Whistler Mountain, large glaciers and glacial lakes can be seen at a distance. Closer views are available from Garibaldi Lake, Wedgemount Lake, and Upper Joffre Lake. Here, glaciers push their melting snow into emerald lakes. All three areas are popular with mountaineers.

Helicopter or floatplane flights are also good for glacier-viewing. Warning: do not venture on or below glaciers without proper instruction and equipment.

You won't feel crowded skiing Blackcomb Mountain's Horstman Glacier, approximately 45 hectares in total area. To get to Horstman, ride from Blackcomb Base to Mile High Station at the top of Seventh Heaven Express. The glacier is serviced by two T-bars.

Other facts

- Top elevation: 2330 metres
- Lift-serviced vertical: 209 metres
- Exposure: northwest
- Terrain: extremely varied
- Skier level: novice to experienced
- Travel time from valley: 45 minutes

Summer skiing and hiking on the mountains

SUBSTANTIAL WINTER snowfalls translate into ideal summer skiing on Blackcomb Mountain, the only ski resort in North America to offer lift-serviced public summer glacier skiing. From mid-June to early August, the mountain's Horstman Glacier offers spring-like snow conditions with comfortably warm temperatures.

Routes to the top

- **Whistler Mountain's** fully enclosed 10-passenger Whistler Village Gondola operates from June to mid-October, carrying sightseers and mountain bikers to the Roundhouse and an alpine world 1157 metres above the Village. Trails to alpine lakes pass through meadows carpeted with wildflowers. Visitors can hike or bike. Twice a day, a free, guided orientation tour is offered from the top of the Whistler Gondola.

- **Blackcomb Mountain's** open-air quad chairlift with optional bubble cover leaves from the daylodge at the base of Blackcomb. Travel to Rendezvous Lodge, or take the bus beyond to the Seventh Heaven Chair for the panoramic views. Marked trails for

Summer skiing on Blackcomb's Horstman Glacier

hikers and bikers lead to alpine meadows and woods. Guided nature tours of the Glacier Cave are free.

Trails can lead to a leisurely stroll or energetic hike

Easy adventures

Not all activities in the Whistler area require super-athletic abilities. Some, like sightseeing and flightseeing, don't require any at all.

Tip: if you're starting out with a new sport such as in-line skating, sailing, or tennis, you can arrange lessons through the Whistler Activity and Information Centre or by calling the following companies direct.

Valley tours

Sit back and enjoy air-conditioned bus comfort with lunches and commentary. Whistler Resort and the surrounding area can be seen with one of the following guiding companies. Multilingual guides are available upon request. For a special treat, try a luxurious classic car tour. Book by calling Classic Car Tours at 932-2259. Bus tours are hosted by the following:
- Japanada: 932-2685
- Whistler Nature Guide: 932-4595
- Playguide Tours: 938-9688
- Whistler Guide Service: 938-1167

Flightseeing

Getting above it all in a helicopter, floatplane, or glider is a memorable way to sightsee. Below are spacious valleys, looming mountains, cathedral peaks, emerald-green alpine lakes, dormant volcanoes, and countless glaciers.

Glider rides—with a best glide speed of 90 kilometres per hour—are offered from April through October by the Pemberton Soaring Centre at Pemberton Airport. Pilots are licensed by the Department of Transport, after many hours of soaring experience. The company also offers a training program.

Flights may be booked through the Whistler Activity and Information Centre or directly with the companies

Mountain schedules

Whistler Mountain

Summer operations are in effect from early June to mid-October. The Whistler Activity and Information Centre has trail maps and campsite information. Lift tickets can be booked through the Whistler Activity and Information Centre or purchased from the mountain base in Whistler Village. For more information, call 932-2394.

Blackcomb Mountain

Summer sightseeing operations are in effect from early June to early September. Summer skiing and snowboarding run to early August and are dependent on weather conditions. Lift tickets and lessons can be purchased through Blackcomb Guest Relations or at the daylodge at the base of Blackcomb Mountain. Contact Blackcomb Guest Relations at 932-3141/ 687-1032.

listed below. Scenic glacier tours, landings, heli-picnics, backcountry skiing, and snowshoeing are options.

- Alpine Adventure Tours: 932-2705/683-6037
- Blackcomb Helicopters: 938-1700
- Canadian Helicopters: 276-7663; Fax: 278-1637
- Glacier Air Tours: 898-9016 (Squamish), 932-2705 (Whistler), 683-0209 (Vancouver)
- Mountain Heli-Sports: 932-2070; Fax: 938-1852
- Pemberton Soaring Centre: 894-5727/589-0653
- Tyax Heli-Skiing & Heli-Hiking: 932-7007; Fax: 932-2500
- Western Canadian Heli-Sports: 938-1700
- Whistler Air: 932-6615; Fax: 932-6100
- Whistler Helicopters: 932-3512
- Whistler Heli-Skiing & Hiking: 932-4105
- The Whistler Outdoor Experience Company: 932-3389; Fax: 932-4469

In-line skating

Although in-line skating is the fastest-growing recreational pastime in North America, not all skaters in Whistler are cruising around gazing at the scenery. Many residents use the resort's network of paved trails, roads, and parking lots to get to and from work. Insider's tip: local in-line skaters try new moves in the Fitzsimmons Creek Skateboarding Park, just north of the Whistler Village day ski parking lot.

Whether you're an experienced skater or a family starting out together, high-quality, low-cost in-line skating clinics at Blackcomb Ski & Sport (at the base of the Wizard) will keep you in line. Call 938-7788 for information and clinic times. Other rental and retail locations for in-line skating equipment include:

- Can-Ski: 932-1975/938-7744
- Excess Clothing & Accessories: 932-2224
- McCoo's Excessive Accessories: 932-2823; bikes, too
- Sports West: 938-7777
- Whistler Blades: 932-9669

Tennis

Public and private courts dot the Whistler Valley. Many free courts are maintained for public use by the Whistler Parks and Recreation Department (938-7275).

As well, local hotels such as the Chateau Whistler (938-8000) let you bat a ball. The Delta Mountain Inn has covered tennis courts; same-day bookings only. Call 932-1982 for rates and times. The newest member of the tennis set, the Whistler Racquet & Golf Resort (932-1991/938-8091), will ultimately have 10 tennis courts, including 3 covered courts and a stadium court for tennis

exhibitions.

Frequent visitors as well as local residents have swelled membership and drop-in use of the Whistler Valley Tennis Club on Lake Placid Road (938-3138). A community-based summer club, it has five courts and a clubhouse, which are open from May 1 to mid-October. Because it is a non-profit society, membership fees are rock-bottom: $140 for first-time members, $125 for adult renewals, $30 for juniors 13–17, and children under 12 free with adult sign-up. There are no court fees.

Horseback riding/hayrides

Horseback riding tours take you through Pemberton Meadows, 35 kilometres north of Whistler, or along trails around the Whistler area. For an authentic Western experience, take a chuckwagon ride through open fields and stay in teepee accommodations. Some tours combine adventures—for example, a morning rafting trip on the Lillooet River with a haywagon or horseback ride after lunch.

Booking water-related activities

TO BOOK WATER-RELATED activities, contact the following:

- Lillooet Jet Inc.: 938-0411/ 894-5237 (jet boating)
- Cayoosh Expeditions: 894-5502 (kayaking, rafting)
- Sea to Sky Kayaking School: 898-5498 (kayaking)
- Tyax Heli-Hiking: 932-7007 (canoeing, jet boating, river rafting)
- Wedge Rafting: 932-7171 (whitewater and float rafting)
- Whistler Jet Boating: 932-3389/894-5200 (jet boating)
- Whistler River Adventures: 932-3532 (whitewater and float rafting)
- The Whistler Outdoor Experience Company: 932-3389; Fax: 932-4469 (jet boating, canoeing, kayaking, windsurfing)
- Whistler Sailing & Water Sports: 932-7245 (sailing, canoeing, kayaking)

Evenings often include bonfires and sing-alongs.

- Black Tusk Adventures-Mountain Tours: 932-8749
- Chilcotin Horseback Adventures: 238-2274 (phone/fax)
- Layton Bryson Outfitting and Trail Riding: 932-6623
- McLeod Creek Wilderness Ranch: 894-5704/894-6944
- Tyax Heli-Hiking: 932-7007; Fax: 932-2500
- Tyax Mountain Lake Resort: 238-2221; Fax: 238-2528
- Western Adventures on Horseback: 894-6155/894-6968
- Wild Country Horse Safari: 894-5680
- The Whistler Outdoor Experience Company: 932-3389; Fax: 932-4469

Paintball

Whistler Paintball Adventures offers an alternative to traditional team sports. Most players prefer the standard version of Capture the Flag, locating and retrieving the opposing team's flag while defending their own and avoiding being painted. Call 932-3524 to book your group.

Lakes and parks

Five lakes and seven parks dot the Whistler Valley, offering ample opportunity to swim, boardsail, canoe, kayak, sail, water-ski, fish, or just relax and soak up the sun on a beach. All lakes are accessible from the Valley Trail network that winds through Whistler.

The River of Golden Dreams, originally dubbed the River of Golden Dreams and Romance by pioneer resort owner Alex Philip, runs from the north end of Alta Lake along the Valley Trail and crosses Highway 99 before joining Green Lake. This link between the two lakes makes an ideal route for a quiet canoe or kayak tour.

Water-related activities

Each of Whistler Valley's five lakes—Alpha, Nita, Alta, Lost, and Green—have park, beach, and picnic facilities.

Alta Lake, once known as Summit Lake, is the highest body of water in the Whistler Valley. From its south end, water flows to Howe Sound. From the north end, water flows to the ocean by way of the Lillooet and Fraser rivers. Local lakes once teemed with fish, making the area a popular summer holiday destination. Today all of Whistler's five lakes are stocked to keep numbers up.

Alta Lake is well serviced with canoe, kayak, windsurfer, and sailboat rentals. You can take a 30-minute paddle across Alta Lake and down the River of Golden Dreams with return transportation and refreshments provided or a two-hour canoe or kayak trip down the same river. The unspoiled wetlands along the route make for excellent bird-watching.

Scenic boat tours, waterskiing, whitewater rafting, and jet boat packages from half-day to three days are offered on the Green, Birkenhead, Lillooet, Elaho, and Thompson rivers.

Parks

Each of the seven parks in the Whistler Valley is free to visitors, with rentals and packages also available. The parks are Alpha Lake, Wayside, Lakeside, Rainbow, Meadow, Emerald, Dream River, Green Lake, and Lost Lake.

Columbia ground squirrels

NATURE GUIDE STEPHANE Perron of Whistler Nature Guide has lived in the area for more than a decade. "Always be prepared when travelling in the wilderness," he advises. "Seek advice from knowledgeable people. Leave wilderness as wild as can be after you have gone through." Another tip from Stephane: wildlife viewing is always best in the early hours of the morning.

Here Stephane shares his observations of what to look for in the Whistler area from April to October.

April

The ice on our valley lakes begins to break up. Trumpeter swans stop in for a week or two on their migration north. You may see them on shallow lake shores, such as the south end of Green Lake, where they feed on water vegetation. They are shy animals, so bring binoculars if you want to get a good look.

BC has one of the largest concentrations of hummingbirds, and they now return from wintering in South America. You are sure to see one hovering where people have installed nectar feeders. Look for skunk cabbage heads piercing through the snow in wetland areas. You can't miss their distinctive odour.

May

May is the water month. When the snow melts, there's no end to the waterfalls and mountain streams. In the shallow waters of Alta Lake near Rainbow Park and the south shore of Lost Lake, thousands of tadpoles dart in the water, forming large black moving masses. Hike to the Giant Cedars, a remote grove of red cedars more than 1000 years old. Some are over 3 metres in diameter. The trail passes lakes, streams, lush plant life, and berries late in the season. Closer to home and with easier access, are large Douglas–firs behind Alpha Lake Park. Sitka spruce and cedars are found down a small trail between the railway track and the pedestrian bridge crossing the bridge at the bottom of Lorimer Road.

Although mountain goats are shy creatures, they can be seen within the Black Tusk Nature Conservancy, on the south face of Wedge Mountain, and across the Green River at Nairn Falls Park. Car viewing of mountain goats is often possible from February to May on the Squamish River Road, about 2 kilometres above Ashlu Creek. In northern areas, moose graze along shorelines at nightfall. Binoculars are a must.

June

Most forest flowers bloom this month. A walk down any forest trail reveals carpets of dwarf dogwood (the provincial flower), queen's cup, columbine, and Indian paintbrush. Wild strawberries are found in many sunny exposed patches, and delicious farm strawberries are ready for picking in Pemberton. Located below Whistler, Pemberton is in a large, flat valley and has a warmer, drier climate. Dim daylight can be seen as late as 11:30 pm. Ice on alpine lakes begins to break up.

For bird-watching, try the nature refuge established within the Whistler town limits at the confluence of 21 Mile and Alta creeks. The north end of Alta Lake near Rainbow Park and the south end of Green Lake are good for viewing colourful birds such as warblers, woodpeckers, hummingbirds, and even ospreys and great blue herons. A paddle down the River of Golden Dreams is recommended for spotting grebes, geese, and beavers. Beavers also swim in the evening around the western shores of Alpha and Alta lakes.

Whistler and Blackcomb lifts are the most likely places to see black bears. Occasionally seen are deer, coyotes, and bobcats. Small mammals in the area include rabbits, beavers, weasels, and squirrels. Ptarmigan, pikas, and marmots live in alpine areas above the treeline. On Whistler Mountain, you'll likely spot hoary marmots sunning themselves on rocks.

July

By mid-July, most alpine regions are free of snow for hiking. Alpine wildflowers blossom in showy array during their short season from the end of July to early August. The meadows on Whistler Mountain, especially on the early flowering sections of the Musical Bumps, are recommended, as are Black Tusk meadows just beyond Garibaldi Lake. The Brandywine meadows are not as popular but offer

Black bear

Mule deer

some of the best wildflower displays. Rainbow Lake has a small area but is another good choice.

In the valley, plants that flowered last month are now showing their berries. Look to the night sky for the most dramatic views of the Milky Way.

August

This is the month to go berry picking. Large blue huckleberries and red raspberries, favourite foods of black bears, are now abundant. Most of the snow has melted off the glaciers, exposing massive crevasses and seracs. It's a good time to see them, either hiking or on a scenic mountain flight.

On the Gates and Birkenhead rivers north of Whistler, thousands of red Pacific sockeye salmon begin to make their way upriver to spawn.

The trail to Cheakamus Lake leads through an oldgrowth forest to a glacier setting. Large, mature trees, thick moss, and forest life typical of West

Coyote

Coast old-growth forests are seen here. A cable car lifts you over the glacial Cheakamus River.

September

Thousands of spawning salmon travel up the Gates and Birkenhead rivers from late August to early October. In September, they are at their peak. View from many spots along the Squamish and Cheakamus river systems. A nature trail at the outlet of Alice Lake permits observation of fish spawning beds.

Aspen leaves turn to yellows and golds as the season ends.

October to May

October brings cooler, wetter days. Mushrooms pop up everywhere, including edible pine and chanterelle varieties. By late November, bald eagles begin gathering in Brackendale, south of Whistler, to feast on the dying chum salmon.

For nature tours, contact the following:

Whistler Nature Guide: 932-4595 (phone/fax)

The Whistler Outdoor Experience Company: 932-3389; Fax: 932-4469

Hiking provides scenery, exercise and an affordable way to get around

BOTH WHISTLER and Blackcomb mountains coordinate extensive summer sightseeing, hiking, and biking programs in the high alpine areas. Mountain trails are marked and vary in difficulty from novice to expert. Most ages can enjoy the beauty and freshness of high alpine environments. Choose the hike best suited to the experience, degree of physical fitness, and age range of your group.

You can also hike with a guiding company, join a mountain bike tour, or enjoy free naturalist's walks courtesy of the mountains.

Whistler Mountain summer trails

All tours, nature walks, hikes, and mountain bike excursions begin at the Roundhouse after a 25-minute ride aboard the Whistler Village Gondola. The Harmony Express Gondola began operations in December 1994, opening up new alpine areas for the summer of 1995. A map with detailed trail information is available from Whistler Mountain as well as from the Whistler Activity and Information Centre.

Trails from the Roundhouse:
Harmony Meadows
• Level: Challenging
• Return distance: 2.6 kilometres
• Time: 30–60 minutes
• Elevation change: 50 metres

Harmony Lake Trail
• Level: Somewhat challenging
• Return distance: 2 kilometres to Harmony Lake, 3.5 kilometres around Harmony Loop
• Time: 60–90 minutes
• Elevation change: 100 metres
• Open meadows, alpine forests, and lakes; views of Fitzsimmons Valley, Overlord Mountain and Glacier

Low Harmony Lake Loop (Extension of Harmony Lake Trail)
• Level: Easier
• Return distance: 0.6 kilometres from Harmony Loop
• Time: 15 minutes
• Elevation Change: 25 metres
• Explore unique alpine tarns sculpted by glaciers and snow/water runoff

Glacier Trail
• Level: Somewhat challenging
• Return distance: 2.5 kilometres
• Time: 60 minutes
• Elevation change: 150 metres

Ridge Lookout Trail
• Level: Somewhat challenging
• Return distance: 1.2 kilometres
• Time: 30–35 minutes
• Elevation change: 85 metres
• A short, steep hike that terminates at a lookout; views include Cayley, Powder, Rainbow, Wedge, and Overlord mountains, and Harmony Lakes.

Paleface Trail
• Level: Somewhat challenging
• Return distance: 1 kilometre around loop
• Time: 20–30 minutes
• Elevation change: 85 metres
• A gentle trail with views of two extinct volcanoes, Mt. Fee and Mt. Cayley. Sit and enjoy the scenery on several benches.

Musical Bumps Trail to Singing Pass
• Level: Challenging hike (for serious, well-prepared hikers)
• Return distance: 19 kilometres, 25 kilometres to Whistler Village
• Time: 5–6 hours
• Elevation change: Several; 152-305 metres
• Top-of-the-world views of Black Tusk, Overlord Mountain, Cheakamus Glacier, and Cheakamus Lake.

Blackcomb Mountain summer trails

Tours, nature walks, hikes, and mountain bike excursions begin at the top of the Wizard Express or the Solar Coaster Express.

Lifts run from mid-June to early September. A map with detailed trail information is available from Blackcomb Mountain as well as the Whistler Activity and Information Centre. Choose from the following hiking trails:

Rendezvous Loop
• Novice circuit
• Length: 0.75 kilometres
• Vertical drop: 65 metres
• Estimated time: 30 minutes
• Start/Finish: Rendezvous Restaurant
• A gentle walk meanders through the tree line on Rendezvous Ridge.

Treeline Trail
• Intermediate circuit
• Length (one way): 1.5 kilometres
• Vertical drop: 80 metres
• Estimated time (one way): 60–90 minutes
• Start/finish: Rendezvous Restaurant/Blackcomb Lake
• Hike follows Summit Trail uphill from Rendezvous Restaurant. Once the trail flattens out 0.75 kilometres above the Rendezvous, you'll see the new 57-million-litre snowmaking reservoir. From this point, the Treeline Trail follows the natural benches in the terrain, passing under the Seventh Heaven Chair and through alpine meadows. Final destination is Blackcomb Lake. From here, follow the Lakeside Trail uphill to the Summit Trail and back to Rendezvous.

Summit Trail
• Expert circuit
• Length: 5 kilometres
• Vertical drop: 350 metres
• Estimated time: 2–2.5 hours
• Start/Finish: Rendezvous Restaurant
• Follow the Summit Trail to Horstman Hut for lunch and panoramic view. Then follow the Summit Trail downhill to the Lakeside Trail to Blackcomb Lake. From here, take the Treeline Trail back to Rendezvous.

Have a safe hike

GO SLOWLY UNTIL you acclimatize to mountain altitudes. Mile High Station on Blackcomb Mountain, for example, is 2284 metres above sea level. You may experience shortness of breath and tire more easily. Plan short trips until you get in shape.

Weather can change abruptly and unexpectedly in the mountains. Think ahead to avoid serious sunburn, the danger of hypothermia, or injury.

The sun's rays are 30 percent stronger at 2134 metres than at sea level. Liberally apply sunscreen protection on exposed skin. Good sunglasses, a hat, and a full bottle of water are mandatory.

Adequate clothing is also a must. Jackets or sweaters are advised for adults and children. Even if hot weather reigns down below, it can be on the cold, windy side up above. Expect as much as a 5°C temperature differential between lift base and mountain destination. Check with ticket offices for up-to-date weather information.

Good walking shoes or sneakers, not high heels, are recommended. Getting on and off the lifts is that much easier. As well, sturdy shoes reduce the possibility of tripping on loose rocks on mountain trails.

Hiking trails are rated for time and distance and are patrolled. Follow the signs and stay on hiking trails to avoid damaging the fragile alpine vegetation. Do not ride or hike on ski trails. Even one track or footprint on a ski trail can start damaging water erosion.

Observe all boundary signs and area closures, particularly areas of lift construction and slope preparation. Steep slopes, snowfields and ice fields are also areas to avoid. When you leave, be sure to pack out all of your garbage.

Hiking trails become available as snow recedes. Please check trail status with mountain staff. In case of emergency, use phones located at lift huts. Dial O to summon aid.

A DEDICATED GROUP of local enthusiasts is responsible for the tremendous growth of mountain biking along the Sea to Sky corridor. Working together, the Squamish Off-Road Cycling Association, the Squamish Trail Society, and the Whistler Off-Road Cycling Association have developed trails within Squamish, Alice Lake Provincial Park, Whistler, and Birkenhead. Bikers also tackle Highway 99, the best of them cycling to and from Vancouver in a day. The undulating highway between Whistler and Mount Currie and beyond, along the Pemberton Portage Road to Anderson Lake, also sees its share of mountain bikers, riding solo or in organized groups. A caution to road bikers: cycle with extreme care; wear your helmet and bright colours. Speeding is common on Highway 99. If possible, avoid highway riding on weekends.

The Sea to Sky Trail

A 300-kilometre mountain bike route, the Sea to Sky Trail, will eventually take riders of all ages and abilities from Squamish as far as Seton Portage. A 60-kilometre trail between Squamish and Whistler that winds beside lakes, past waterfalls, across rivers, through canyons, and around mountains is already open.

Beginning at the Squamish Estuary, the trail starts out fairly flat along the dyke parallel to the Squamish River. Riders then travel northbound to the end of Government Road, taking a left to Fergie's Lodge. Crossing a bridge,

cyclists head right towards the Outdoor School. After the paved road ends, a gravel road leads over BC Rail tracks and two bridges before narrowing into a trail. This is the start of Paradise Valley, a bike route meandering beside Starvation Lake. A gradual climb leads to great views of the Tantalus Range. At the lookout on Highway 99, riders continue on the west side of the highway on the gravel portion next to the meridian. Past the salt sheds, take the first road on the east side. A very rideable single-track route leads past Deadman's Lake. The trail ends at the 2.2-kilometre mark, where riders take the road to the left and rejoin Highway 99.

A short distance beyond is the Cheakamus River logging bridge on the west side. Cross the bridge and railway tracks to the gravel road on the right. After passing a yellow gate, cyclists continue along a pleasant stretch past Lucille and Shadow lakes to the Pinecrest Estates subdivision. Another section of highway riding takes cyclists to Brandywine Falls. Travel off-road through the forest, across a suspension bridge at Cal-Cheak campsite, and along old logging roads to the dump site in Whistler. From near sea level in Squamish, bikers climb to 675 metres at Whistler.

For more information, contact the Sea to Sky Trail Society, c/o Sea to Sky Enterprise Centre, Box 2539, Squamish, BC V0N 3G0; telephone: 892-5467; Fax: 892-5227.

Garibaldi Provincial Park

Mountain biking is allowed in two locations in Garibaldi Provincial Park. Try the Diamond Head area at the south end of the park and ride to Elfin Lakes. The Cheakamus Lake Trail leads to Cheakamus Lake. All other trails, including the Rubble Creek and Singing Pass trails, are closed to cyclists for the safety of hikers or for the protection of the fragile alpine environment.

For more information, contact Garibaldi Provincial Park, P.O. Box 220, Brackendale, BC V0N 1H0 (898-3678) and the Whistler Infocentre, Box 181, Whistler, BC V0N 1B0 (932-5528).

Whistler Valley

The Whistler area offers excellent mountain bike terrain. On the west side of Highway 99 there are several challenging areas where logging roads provide good access. Remember that logging roads are used by logging trucks. Ride with care.

In addition to bike trails on Whistler and Blackcomb mountains, try the Valley Trail System. A largely paved cycling trail, it winds its way around Whistler, circling Lost Lake and skirting Green, Alta, Nita, and Alpha lakes. The trail is mainly flat, ideal for a relaxed cycle and family touring. The Lost Lake section is 15 kilometres of eight interconnected paved and gravel scenic paths.

For more information on Whistler Valley bike trails, call the Whistler Activity and Information Centre at 932-2394.

Guided tours/hard adventures

"Roads less travelled" certainly describes much of British Columbia. The province is famous for its remote backcountry, rural, and mountain areas. Some regions can only be visited in a four-wheel-drive vehicle; others, such as Lake Lovely Water Recreation Area or the peak of Blackcomb Mountain, are accessible only on foot. Horseback riding is the solution in some cases, whereas in others, standard automobiles can make the grade.

Most packages can be booked through the Whistler Activity and Information Centre, or directly through the companies listed below:
- Black Tusk Adventures Mountain Tours: 932-8749
- Cayoosh Expeditions: 894-5502
- Chilcotin Holidays: 238-2274 (phone/fax)
- Tyax Mountain Lake Resort: 238-2221; Fax: 238-2528
- Whistler Alpine Guides Bureau: 938-3338; Fax: 938-1225
- Whistler Backcountry Adventures: 938-1410
- The Whistler Outdoor Experience Company: 932-3389; Fax: 932-4469

Mountain high

The lure of the Coast Mountains, the highest overall mountain range in Canada, is strong, extending beyond Whistler and Blackcomb mountains. Hiking, rock climbing, and mountain travel during any season is popular; the list of mountain adventures in the Whistler area continues to grow. From novice to experienced participant, you'll find something appropriate to your level of fitness and ability.

Hiking in
Well-marked hiking trails lead into Garibaldi Provincial Park from four access points. The park, a 195 000-hectare mountain wilderness, is noted for its geological history. Volcanic action resulted in the formation of many of the park's peaks, including the Black Tusk, Price Mountain, the Table, Mount Garibaldi, Cinder Cone, and the Glacier Pikes. Lava spewing from Price Mountain created the Barrier, a natural dam behind which Garibaldi Lake was formed. The most famous of the volcanic peaks is surely Black Tusk. Its distinctive appearance is the result of intensive erosion.

Another vast wilderness accessible only by hiking in is the Joffre Lakes Recreation Area. For more on trekking in Garibaldi Provincial Park, see page 41; for Joffre Lakes Recreation Area, see page 137.

Mountaineering
Certified by the BC Association of Mountain Guides, the Whistler Alpine Guides Bureau (938-3338) offers one-day tours as well as mountain skills

Mountain biking

Guided bike tours
- Whistler Backroads Mountain Bike Adventures: 932-3111; Fax: 932-1204
- Fat Tire Adventure Company: 932-2394
- The Whistler Outdoor Experience Company: 932-3389; Fax: 932-4469

Mountain bike rentals
- Whistler Backroads Mountain Bike Adventures: 932-3111; Fax: 932-1204
- Bikestop: 932-3659
- Blackcomb Ski & Sport: 932-7788
- Climb High Cycles: 938-1446
- CanSki Glacier Lodge: 938-7744
- CanSki Whistler Village: 932-1975
- Excess Clothing & Accessories: 932-2224
- McConkey Sport Shop: 932-2311
- McCoo's Excessive Accessories: 932-2823
- Pumphouse Fitness Centre: 932-1984
- Sea to Sky Cycling: 938-1233
- Seymour Cycle & Sport: 932-6026
- Single Track Cycles: 932-6700
- Sportstop: 932-5495
- Sports West: 938-7777
- Whistler Gifts & Sports: 932-1918
- Whistler Village Sports: 932-3327

Off-road cycling etiquette

SAFETY FIRST.
- Watch for hazards and wear a helmet.
- Always control your speed.
- Stay on designated trails.
- Leave no trace.
- Don't shortcut switchbacks.
- Minimize brake slides and skidding.
- Never spook animals; stop and move downslope of horse riders.
- Respect other users.

courses for aspiring crag-climbers of all skill levels. Winter courses include mountain skills, avalanche awareness, glacier travel, and snow camping. Summer skiing day tours include a ski traverse across the Blackcomb Glacier toward Blackcomb and Spearhead col, a Whistler Mountain Symphony Bowl ski toward Singing Pass, and a helicopter-assisted Black Tusk ski tour. From June to October, hikers can join the company for a day hike to the top of Blackcomb Peak. Other backcountry hiking trips and climbing lessons can be arranged.

Hiking in the backcountry can result in unexpected pleasures

The Escape Route (938-3338; Fax: 938-1225) also organizes climbing and mountaineering tours and sells related equipment.

Rock climbing

Begin your rock climbing career with a course aptly called Basic Rock. In addition, Squamish-based Pacific High Mountain Guides (892-5859/ 892-9662) offers instruction all the way from multi-pitch climbing and direct aid climbing to high-angle rescue systems, glacier travel and crevasse rescue, and complete mountaineering. Courses run from April to mid-October. The Tantalus Range, the Wedgemount Lake area, and the Joffre Group are the high points of the Sea to Sky corridor. Guided trips into these and other alpine areas are available upon request. Tyax Heli-Hiking (932-7007; Fax:

932-2500) also offers rock climbing and mountaineering courses.

Mini-treks

The Whistler area abounds with hiking trails. Many, like the Cheakamus Lake Trail, are short, easy hikes through old-growth forests. Entrance to the trail's access road is 7.5 kilometres south of Whistler Village. Another 8.5 gravelled kilometres leads to the 3.2-kilometre Cheakamus Lake trail. Enroute, take a short diversion to the cable car across the Cheakamus River.

Another relatively easy hike is to Giant Cedars (also known as Ancient Cedars and Cougar Mountain Cedars). The grove of 1000-year-old cedars and 650-year-old Douglas-firs is worth a visit. Nine kilometres past Whistler Village at the north end of Green Lake, follow the gravel logging road on the left to the Giant Cedars trail. Try driving in, if your car is up to it, or hike in. If you drive part way, park your car

well off the logging road. The hike is a 12-kilometre round trip from Highway 99, 4 kilometres return from the end of the logging road.

Easy hiking tours into the mountains are a specialty of the Whistler Outdoor Experience Company (932-3389). A mini-trek into Garibaldi Provincial Park's alpine region starts from the summit of the Whistler Mountain Gondola. The eight-hour return trek includes glaciers, alpine lakes, wildflower meadows, a picnic lunch, and refreshments. A three-hour return safari to the volcanic formations of the Black Tusk alpine area is also offered.

Freshwater fishing

Every year, more than 556,000 anglers cast their lines in BC waterways and a total of 4,554,990 days are spent fishing. About 25 percent of BC's anglers are visitors from outside the province. More than half of these visit just to fish.

Of the 72 species of fish

found in BC, 22 are considered sport fish. Two stand out as the most sought after by anglers—salmon in the tidal waters of the coast and rainbow trout in the freshwater lakes and rivers of interior BC. More than three-fifths of all freshwater anglers in BC are after trout of one kind or another. Rainbow trout alone comprise half of the 4.4 million freshwater fish reeled in each year. Each year, BC Fisheries supplies more than 1000 lakes and streams with 12 million young fish, including several species of trout.

More than 85 percent of BC fishing takes place between April and September.

Whistler was a fishing resort long before it became famous for its skiing. In the Sea to Sky area, rainbow trout, Dolly Varden char, cutthroat, brook trout, kokanee, and, in season, salmon, and steelhead, predominate. Spring (February to May) is recommended for steelhead, chinook salmon, and trout; April to October for rainbow trout, kokanee, cutthroat, and Dolly Varden; fall (September to November) for coho salmon, rainbow trout, and Dolly Varden.

Where the action is

Enroute to Whistler, a 3.2-kilometre trail through old-growth forest leads to Cheakamus Lake in Garibaldi Provincial Park. Rainbow trout fishing with fly or spin gear is recommended where the Cheakamus River leaves the lake. In the fully serviced Alice Lake Provincial Park, Alice, Fawn, Edith, and Stump lakes yield rainbow and brook trout, cutthroat, and Dolly Varden.

Northwest of Pemberton, in Birkenhead Lake Provincial Park, is the best kokanee fishing in the area. Rainbow and Dolly Varden and a number of non-salmonid fish, including whitefish, are also caught here. In the Gold Bridge area, a number of lakes, including Tyaughton, Carpenter, and Gun, are stocked with kokanee, rainbow, and Dolly Varden.

In the Whistler area, five local lakes (Alpha, Nita, Alta, Lost, and Green), several winding rivers, and countless streams tempt anglers. All local lakes are stocked. Tour companies provide professional guides and fishing packages that include hotel pickup, equipment, and coaching. Novice and experienced anglers are equally welcome.

Many lakes and rivers in

Off-road excursions

FOUR-WHEEL-DRIVE and ATV (all-terrain vehicle) packages will also get you into the backcountry. Whistler ATV (932-6681) conducts its tours in the Brandywine Falls/Cheakamus Valley area. Whistler Backcountry Adventures (938-1410) also runs guided ATV and four-wheel-drive programs.

Go it by jeep with Black Tusk Adventures (932-8749) four-wheel-drive mountain tours. Half-day, three-hour tours feature mountain trails through Garibaldi Provincial Park and Native reservations. Professional Western guides, knowledgeable in local nature lore, come with the package. Real cowboy cooking over an open fire, live Western entertainment, oil lanterns, and checkered linens hark back to pioneer ranching days.

Highway 99's lakes and rivers provide ample fishing opportunities

the area are not accessible by main roads. Four-wheel-drive vehicles or trucks are required for travel along some gravel roads and former logging roads. For others, the only way in is on foot. Obey all signs and warnings when travelling off road. Very real avalanche danger has closed some areas.

BC Fishing Adventures, a guide to freshwater fishing in the Lower Mainland (available from Infomap, 2647 Anscomb Place, Victoria, BC V8R 2C7) and *BC Fishing's* annual *Freshwater Directory and Atlas* (BC Outdoors, 202–1132 Hamilton Street, Vancouver, BC V6B 2S2) are two useful publications.

Licenses are required to fish in BC. Buy yours at Whistler Hardware (932-3863), Whistler Village Sports (932-3327), Whistler Backcountry Adventures (938-1410), and McKeever's General Store (932-3600). For information about freshwater fishing, consult the *BC Fishing and Hunting Regulations*, the Fish and Wildlife Conservation officer

in Squamish (892-5971), or the Squamish base of the Department of Fisheries and Oceans (892-3230). Since four-wheel-drive vehicles can damage spawning channels, check with the above before crossing streams in your vehicle. To report fisheries-related violations, call 1-800-465-4336.

Fishing tours normally run between April and November, often to remote alpine lakes. Whether you prefer to drive in, fly in, or hike in, book through the Whistler Activity and Information Centre or call direct:
• Whistler Backcountry Adventures: 938-1410; Fax: 932–2500
• Chilcotin Fishing Adventures 238-2274 (phone/fax)
• Tyax Heli-Hiking: 932-7007; Fax: 932-2500
• Tyax Mountain Lake Resort: 238-2221; Fax: 238-2528
• Western Canadian Heli-Sports: 938-1700
• Whistler Air Wilderness Fishing: 932-6615
• Whistler Fishing Guides: 932-4267

Backcountry gear checklist

WEATHER IS CHANGEABLE in the backcountry. Days can be hot, nights cold, especially at the higher elevations you are likely to encounter here. Depending on the tour, you may need all or nearly all of the following items. The list is also useful if you're travelling independently:
❑ Warm sleeping bag
❑ Tent
❑ Rain pants and jackets (no ponchos)
❑ Comfortable pants or jeans
❑ Warm down or wool jacket
❑ Long johns
❑ Lightweight stretchy shorts
❑ Two pairs of gloves
❑ Five pairs of light to medium socks
❑ Toque or headband
❑ Binoculars
❑ Flashlight (check the batteries)
❑ Good camera, spare battery, lots of film
❑ Small day pack or waist pack
❑ Bathing suit
❑ Insect repellent
❑ Sunscreen
❑ Sunglasses
❑ Rubber boots (gum boots)
❑ Towel and face cloth
❑ Biodegradable, unscented toiletries
❑ Medications for allergies, bee and wasp stings
❑ Two complete changes of clothing
For riding trips, include:
❑ Riding boots with heels
❑ Wide-brim Western hat

*Airbound adventurers soar over a
glacier-studded mountain landscape near Whistler*

The Whistler Convention Centre

Conference call

Unbelievable as it may seem, some people do come to Whistler to work. Whistler Resort spotted a market in 1989 when it built the Whistler Conference Centre, located near Village Gate Boulevard after leaving Highway 99 for Whistler Village. This modern, 3252-square-metre facility accommodates conferences, seminars, and workshops for groups of up to 1600 participants. It's also home to the offices of the Whistler Resort Association, Whistler Centre for Business and the Arts, and the Rainbow Theatre, which doubles as a lecture hall for conferences as well as the community's movie house.

The Conference Centre includes the Sea to Sky Ballroom for up to 1600 people in a theatre or reception style. Up to 1000 delegates can dine here. The Rainbow Theatre seats up to 300 people for lectures. Nine conference rooms cater to small groups of under 200 people, and the Atrium, a multilevel landscaped room, hosts receptions or trade shows. An outdoor patio is used for brunches and après-ski dining. Bag lunches are provided for conference participants who sneak away to ski, bike, hike, or laze in the sun during the day.

The Whistler Conference Centre plans and services all meetings and banquets and can organize leisure activities. Over 65 percent of the centre's market is Canadian; the remaining 35 percent is American.

The average conference usually lasts three to four days, but many delegates either book early or stay longer. Some bring their families along.

For more conference or

Whistler Centre for Business and the Arts

LOCATED ON THE upper level of the Whistler Conference Centre is the office of the Whistler Centre for Business and the Arts. Among other programs, the centre offers week-long seminars on managing festivals, resort planning and management, golf course executive management, and ski and study programs. Programs can be custom-designed for individual group needs. The centre also offers cultural programs, such as photography workshops led by renowned nature photographers. Since opening in 1989, over 6000 people have attended the centre's concerts, seminars, and educational forums. For more information, call 932-8310 or 682-5248.

A medley of classical and pop favourites draws impressive crowds

meeting information, call 932-3928 (Whistler) or 631-3032 (Vancouver).

Bar bands and then some

The music scene starts with live entertainment, from the Bourbon Tabernacle Choir to Summer of Love, in bars and lounges, but it doesn't stop there. Jazz to classical, country to cajun, you'll hear it all in the resort, often in outdoor settings. Popular Canadian bands like Bob's Your Uncle are also featured, as well as the Vancouver Symphony Orchestra, the Colorado String Quartet, and jazz great Moe Koffman. As symphony Maestro Sergiu Comissiona observes, "Whistler is a natural place for a summer music festival."

A musical feast is more like it. Since 1989, with the launch of Music in the Mountains, Whistler's musical offerings have grown in stature. The annual week-long Whistler Classical Music Festival, held in mid-August, presents classical music throughout Whistler. Afternoon outdoor performances are held daily from 2:00 pm onward, highlighting small ensembles, including brass, strings, woodwind, and voice. Another annual event, Brass on a Raft, features a brass quintet playing on Lost Lake as a cap to the week.

The Vancouver Symphony Orchestra also visits annually, performing high atop Whistler Mountain with artists like mezzo-soprano Judith Forst.

In the valley, Whistler Resort's Main Stage and an acoustic stage set up in the Black Market at the base of Blackcomb Mountain present free entertainment throughout the summer.

Late in July, take in the Whistler Country and Blues Festival, three days of country blues, rockabilly, country swing, and cajun music on the streets and stages of Whistler. The annual event features more than a dozen bands. Line dancing lessons are offered on the Main Stage, and a chili cook-off is held at the Black Market. The Western weekend ends with a barn dance at the Whistler Conference Centre with a half dozen top country and blues bands.

In mid-September, Whistler hosts the Fall for Jazz Festival. From noon to dusk, all varieties of jazz from 1940s standards to gospel, brass, and bebop are presented on the Main Stage and throughout the resort. The festival attracts top Juno Award-winning musicians and winners of the impressive Montreal Alcan Jazz competition. Groups like the Total Experience Gospel Choir of Seattle also perform.

To top off the summer, late September features Big Band Boom, a weekend of big band music from concert to marching bands. Rain or shine, four bands entertain daily in the Village Square. Some even march down the Village Stroll.

Music in the Mountains

In 1990, the Whistler Centre for Business and the Arts introduced a revolutionary concept: Music in the Mountains,

Brass on a Raft is a highlight of Music in the Mountains

a concert series featuring both internationally known artists and Canada's most talented musicians. "We originally invited world-class musicians on behalf of local audiences. Now people are travelling to Whistler from far afield to hear these and our own local performers," says founder June Goldsmith.

Some ten programs are staged every year. Concerts have featured BC pianists Marc Durrand and Music in the Mountain's Artistic Director Jane Coop performing four-hand music and the sonatas of Haydn and Mozart. An annual event is a performance by the Cornucopia Brass Ensemble of three French horns, trumpet, and two trombones playing music from the Renaissance to the Jazz Age.

In July, pianists taking part in the Whistler Young Artists' Experience also get a chance to shine. Young musical stars, aged 12 to 17, perform the

Canada Day celebrations

CANADA'S BIRTHDAY, July 1, is a big event in Whistler. A main attraction is the annual Canada Day Parade, organized by the Whistler Chamber of Commerce. As one of the parade's organizers, Stan Langtry, puts it, "The parade is a chance to show off the interesting people who live and work in Whistler." The entire resort gets behind the effort, including individuals and more than 30 businesses and community services. You'll see classic cars, flag bearers, street entertainers and clowns, decorated bicycles, musical ensembles, and colourful floats.

The celebration starts at 11:30 am, rain or shine, in Whistler Marketplace Square, with a flag raising. Singers serenade the crowd with a version of "O Canada." And because there are so many US visitors, who celebrate their own country's birthday three days later, both US and Canadian flags are raised. The parade proceeds along Northlands Boulevard, crosses Village Gate, and proceeds through Whistler Village to the base of Blackcomb, where refreshments are served.

likes of Haydn and Mozart for public audiences. For more on this program, see "Whistler for Kids."

For concert information, contact the Whistler Centre for Business and the Arts at 932-8310/682-5248 (toll-free from Vancouver); Fax: 932-4461.

Art smart

In 1990, the first art gallery opened in Whistler. The number has since climbed to six galleries presenting local, national, and international works of art. You are quite likely to meet a working artist on your tour or, at the very least, a knowledgeable gallery manager.

Located in Village Square, the Northwest Connection gallery (932-4646) features works by Canada's foremost Native artists, including carvings, prints, watercolours, jewellery, and masks. Artists such as Salteaux Ojibwa painter Garry Meeches from the Long Plain Six Reserve in Manitoba can be found carving or drawing in the gallery. Drop by to chat and discover the variety and complexity of Native art traditions. Books on Native art can also be purchased. The gallery includes a collection of West Coast designer jewellery in both silver and gold, as well as Baltic amber designed and crafted by master Polish jeweller Josef Banowoski.

The Gaauda Native Fine Arts gallery (932-3382), located in the Chateau Whistler, also offers an impressive selection of Northwest Coast Native art work. Fine wood carvings, masks, painting, sculptures, jewellery, cards, and Native

Galleries display the best of local artists

A rich array of Native art is one of Whistler's strong cultural attractions

music can be purchased here. A large selection of soapstone carvings, including the dancing bears of Kelly Pishicktie, are shown here. Gaauda was named after owner Gina Schubert's Native grandmother. The name means "precious" in the Haida language.

The Shepard Gallery (938-3366), located in St. Andrew's House in Whistler Village, specializes in contemporary art by local, national, and international talents. Among the Canadian artists featured at the gallery are John

Der, Rod Charlesworth, Anne Forman, and Patrick Amiot, who is famous for his whimsical figurative sculptures. The gallery also provides information and books on the major artists it features.

Inge's Gallery Limited (932-6089) is located in the Timberline Lodge. The gallery features the paintings of BC artists such as Pat Audley, Isobel MacLaurin, Janet Young, and Pauline Pike. Original works by Mount Currie painter Rosalie Dipscu, pottery by the team of Daniel

Materna and Zuzy Vacek, and Michael Tickner's colourful paintings are sold along with weaving, glass works, bird houses, jewellery, and cards.

Located in the lower level of the Delta Mountain Inn, the Mountain Craft Gallery (932-5001) features a colourful assortment of fine West Coast crafts. More than 40 BC artists are showcased with works such as quilts, stained glass, wood and metal sculptures, and handmade pine furniture. Stoneware by Charmion Johnson, including garden gargoyles and spotted Appaloosa bowls, are on display. Glass perfume bottles and containers are handcrafted by Morna Tudor.

Also based in the Delta Mountain Inn, the Whistler Village Art Gallery (938-3001) specializes in West Coast artists. Exhibitions showcase Native artists, such as mystical Ojibwa painter Norval Morrisseau, and local artists, such as nature artist Donna-Jane Miller, who is known for her coloured-pencil works. A selection of paintings, prints, jade sculptures, glass work, pottery, country pine antiques, and designer furniture is sold.

The Whistler Village Art Gallery also holds an annual World Cup Art Show during the skiing event.

Isobel MacLaurin, Painter

ISOBEL MACLAURIN'S art is so much a part of Whistler it would be difficult for a visitor to miss one of her creations. Her murals and paintings of landscapes, wildlife, and flowers are displayed at the Roundhouse on Whistler Mountain and in colourful signage along the Valley Trail (one at Alta Lake Road overlooking Nita Lake, six at the interpretive forest, and one at Green Lake), and in Chateau Whistler's logo and Wildflower Café menu. Her portraits include a dual image of Whistler pioneer Myrtle Philip at ages 19 and 95, donated to the new elementary school named in Mrs. Philip's honour.

Born in New Brunswick, Isobel trained as an artist in St. John. After graduating, her first commission was a 9 metre by 2.7 metre mural for an international charity organization. The Roundhouse murals, among her best known, were painted in 1972.

Along with her husband, college instructor Don MacLaurin, Isobel migrated to Whistler when her first child was born. Both Isobel and Don are avid skiers and hikers and have a mutual interest in the local flora and fauna. But

Artist Isobel MacLaurin at work

her love of Whistler has not stopped Isobel from travelling the world in search of subjects; she's sketched in Australia, the islands of the South Pacific, Thailand, Rome, and New Zealand. Her ability to meet and win over "the locals" with her sketches has won her many accolades. "I only need my paints and a sketchbook," she says, "and every door is open. I meet so many exciting and interesting people."

Isobel's home is also her studio. With a spectacular view of Alta Lake and Whistler Mountain, she frequently opens her doors to interested visitors. Exploring her studio, guests view sketches and character portraits from her globe-trotting expeditions: a portrait of a Thai Hill Tribe woman, bursts of alpine flowers, a Polynesian mural, a snow-filled mountain scene, a mother bear with her cubs. Her natural enthusiasm is as infectious as her paintings. For more information or to visit Isobel MacLaurin in her studio, call 932-5324.

Brief encounters

If you tire of working up a sweat, there are other, less physical things to do around Whistler. Not everyone here is mountain-bound 24 hours a day. In addition to live music in lounges and bars, street bands, and Music in the Mountain concerts, there's live theatre performed by the Whistler Summer Theatre (986-4601), free street entertainment throughout the summer months, and the Rainbow Theatre (932-2422), a first-run movie house in the Whistler Conference Centre. Here are some other distractions.

Whistler Museum

Although struggling financially, the Whistler Museum has plans to move its longtime home on Highway 99 to the new Whistler North area. In the meantime, if you spot the museum's open sign on the right-hand side as you travel north (1011 Highway 99 at Function Junction south of Whistler), drop in to view the exhibits on regional history and local personalities. Many,

Live theatre plays a part in Whistler's social life

Picture perfect

IF YOU LOVE photography and want to improve your skills, the Whistler Photography Workshops are the answer. Inspired and patterned after the Maine and Sante Fe photography workshops, participants come from as far away as Newfoundland and New Jersey. A typical day includes rising for a sunrise photo session, followed by a helicopter ride to shoot alpine flowers, followed by a trek to a local waterfall. All in all, a tough way to learn to take photographs.

Held in the summer and fall with the likes of photographers Bryan Peterson, Galen Rowell, Sherman Hines, and Freeman Patterson, as well as BC photographers Sharron Milstein and Paul Lazarski, workshops run from two to five days from July to September. Classroom sessions and field trips capture the many scenic locations and people activities in the Whistler area. Improve your technique and learn about photo design and composition, how to take people shots, and

even how to sell your photos. Hands-on experience and critique sessions are combined.

Donations from several inspired participants have launched a photography collection now displayed inside the Whistler Conference Centre.

For more information, contact the Whistler Centre for Business and the Arts at 932-8310/ 684-5248 (toll-free from Vancouver); Fax: 932-4461.

The streets are alive

DAILY STREET ENTERTAINMENT is launched on Canada's Victoria Day weekend in mid-May and runs to the end of September. Throughout the summer, watch for musicians, jugglers, comedians, magicians, and clowns performing throughout Whistler Resort and on the Main Stage in Village Square.

As many as 20 street-performing individuals or companies congregate for the gregarious Whistler Street Entertainer Festival, held on the Labour Day weekend in September. The festival features the best of Canadian and international entertainers. Cabaret evenings are held on Saturday and Sunday. For more information, contact the Whistler Activity and Information Centre at 932-2394.

Special Days
Continuous summer activities
- Whistler Resort daily summer street entertainment
- Summer Festival Season of Concerts at Whistler Conference Centre
- Whistler Business and the Arts Photography Workshops
- Whistler Summer Theatre

May
- World Technical Skiing Championships on Blackcomb

- Close of Blackcomb Mountain winter ski season
- The Great Snow, Earth & Water Race

June
- Opening of Blackcomb for summer skiing
- Family Days on Whistler Mountain
- Start of summer glacier skiing on Blackcomb Mountain
- Whistler Children's Art Festival
- Commonwealth Fencing Championships
- Alta Lake Fishing Derby

July
- July 1 Canada Day
- Discover Function Junction Days
- Amateur Sailboat Racing Regatta on Alta Lake
- Chateau Whistler Classic Golf Tournament
- Whistler Mountain Swiss Alpine Festival
- Music in the Mountains
- Specialized Cactus Cup Mountain Bike Race
- Whistler Country and Blues Festival
- Whistler Soccer Camps
- National Youth Choir in residence

August
- Porsche Car Club Village Display Day

- Porsche Club Rally Blackmarket at Blackcomb base
- End of summer glacier skiing
- Whistler Classical Music Festival
- Vancouver Symphony Orchestra Mountaintop Concert on Whistler Mountain
- Specialized Mountain Bike Kids Triathlon
- Corvette Club Rally Blackmarket at Blackcomb base
- Alpine Festival

September
- Whistler International Festival of Street Performers
- Alpine Wine Festival on Whistler Mountain
- Whistler Fall for Jazz Festival
- Native Art Show & Sale
- Whistler Cycle Fest
- Cheakamus Challenge Bike Race
- All British Car Run Blackmarket at Blackcomb base
- Big Band Boom in Whistler Village Square
- Whistler Red Hot Bands Weekend

October
- Whistler Village Oktoberfest

November
- Opening day of ski season for Blackcomb and Whistler mountains (US Thanksgiving weekend)

Whistler Brewing Company

THE AVAILABILITY OF crystal clear mountain spring water inspired the Whistler Brewing Company to set up shop at 1209 Alpha Lake Road in Function Junction. Since opening in the fall of 1989, the microbrewery has worked at capacity. It now produces three memorable local beers, the Continental-style Whistler Lager, Black Tusk Ale, a smooth, dark ale with a nutty flavour, and Whistler's Mother Pale Ale. All beers are made using the finest barley malt, hops, yeast, and pure mountain spring water. The beers are available in bottles and on tap in local pubs. The brewing company is open from Tuesday through Friday, 9:00 am to 5:00 pm and on Saturday, 10:00 am to 5:00 pm. Tours run daily from Tuesday through Friday at 2:00 pm and 4:00 pm, as well as Saturday at 2:00 pm. Call 932-6185 for dates and times to view the operation.

Log homes have proved popular in Whistler architecture

like John Millar, were eccentric backcountry characters.

The museum is divided into various areas. A replica of pioneer Myrtle Philip's sitting room at the famous Rainbow Lodge is of particular interest. The local flora and fauna are covered in photographs, and ski country artifacts, such as the original lift sign for Whistler Mountain, are on display. A detailed history of Whistler, written by longtime resident and historian Florence Petersen, presents the complete story of how Whistler grew from a small fishing resort to a big-time ski resort. Call the Whistler Activity and Information Centre at 932-2394 or call 932-7064 for the museum's hours of operation.

Better homes and cabins

Snow Country Magazine named Whistler the world's best overall resort in its 1989 first annual design award. That made Neil Griggs, one of three planning consultants hired by the Municipality of Whistler in 1976, feel as if he'd truly accomplished something.

At the time Griggs was hired, the little community of 600 was growing haphazardly. His mission was to chart a course for future development. Lands, hotels, lifts, golf courses, residential areas, and retail outlets were all taken into consideration.

Expansion mushroomed. The Delta Mountain Inn, the first international hotel chain in the resort, opened in 1980. Lifts were aligned into Whistler Village, and Blackcomb Mountain opened. The Village took shape as a European-style ski resort, with paving-stone pedestrian walkways, lodgings and fine-dining restaurants. Blackcomb Benchlands and Whistler Village North are now being developed.

Despite the thousands of in-and-out international visitors annually, Whistler Resort continues to strengthen its community roots. Balancing the effects of short-term visitors are Whistler Resort's more than 5000 year-round residents. Many others make Whistler a second home during weekends and holidays. Some, like Nancy Greene Raine and husband Al Raine, began building their homes in the late 1970s; others have come to town more recently, with many new homes popping up in the past few years.

If you're intrigued by Whistler's mix of Continental-Coastal architecture, take your car or bike beyond the Village to peek at some of the homes that have made Whistler justifiably famous. Subdivisions are

Every level of Whistler is utilized...from the trails to the skys

available.

"Look for fluorescent," laughs Barry Bateman. "You can recognize paraglider pilots by their fluorescent back packs, shoes, flightsuits, and rip-stop nylon wings. The more colour they wear, the better."

Farther north in the Pemberton Valley, hang-gliding predominates. Between Pemberton and Pemberton Meadows, hang-gliders take to the air between 1:00 pm and 5:00 pm. Heat from the afternoon sun shining on the west side of the mountains creates pleasing soaring conditions.

Although "bi-wingual," Barry prefers hang-gliding. With more than 1000 flights to his credit, he's spent equally as many hours in the air. Novice pilots may remain aloft for as little as 15 seconds. Experts like Barry can stay in the air for up to 12 hours, with a normal long flight ranging from 8 to 10 hours.

For more information, contact the Hang Gliding and Paragliding Association of Canada (HPAC/ACVL) at 888-5090. Also active is the Hang Gliding Association of BC (hang-gliding and paragliding) at 980-9566. The *Western Canadian Site Guide for British Columbia* is available from the above.

YOU'D BE SURPRISED how rarely people look up, says hang-glider pilot Barry Bateman. The devoted administrator of the Hang Gliding and Paragliding Association of Canada (HPAC/ACVL), Barry's been soaring in thermals since 1977.

In that time, he's seen the technical evolution of the sport. Hang-gliding, and its first cousin paragliding, experts say, are now less dangerous than driving a car—if done right, of course. "Most accidents are caused by pure stupidity and lack of professional training," says Barry. "People buy outdated and dangerous equipment at garage sales, then try to teach themselves without knowing what they're doing. It's the HPAC's biggest nightmare."

Hang-gliding and paragliding are closely related, with some significant differences. Hang-gliders, plus related equipment, weigh up to 50 kilograms, including the 6-metre-long aluminum frame and delta-shaped glider. Not surprisingly, they like to drive into launch sites. Paragliders are lighter in weight, under 11 kilograms. With their equipment tucked into a backpack, paraglider pilots can combine a love of hiking with the airborne sport, hiking up a mountain and then sailing down.

In Sea to Sky Country, you might catch a rare glimpse of a paraglider sailing over the Stawamus Chief just south of Squamish. More likely, you'll spot them on Blackcomb Mountain, where the trained instructors of Parawest Paragliding (932-7052) run year-round classes. After lessons, you'll lift off from a glacier to soar above snow-covered runs. Winter sessions require regular ski gear. In the summer, full day and full week packages are

Whistler for Kids

Costumes and kids: a natural match

Local businesses, including Blackcomb and Whistler mountains, have programs and packages designed with families in mind, with discounts and freebies that keep costs down. Just about any type of tour listed in this guidebook can accommodate children. Some, like sleigh rides or

chuck wagon excursions, provide rare opportunities to see the world in old-fashioned ways. In addition to physical activities, children

Fun for kids

Local businesses, including Blackcomb and Whistler mountains, have programs and packages designed with families in mind, with discounts and freebies that keep costs down. Just about any type of tour listed in this guidebook can accommodate children. Some, like sleigh

rides or chuck wagon excursions, provide rare opportunities to see the world in old-fashioned ways. In addition to physical activities, children can learn to paint, go to a play, laugh at the antics of street performers, read books, and learn more about nature and the environment.

During all four seasons, they can choose from active to passive pastimes, from ski lessons to mini-golf, in-line skating to videos.

Myrtle Philip Community Centre

Located on Lorimer Road in Whistler Cay. Information Line: 938-7275.

With the opening of the new Myrtle Philip Community Centre, there's more for families to do than ever before. Two multipurpose rooms, a full gymnasium with a stage, a state-of-the-art computer lab, kitchen, and fireplace lounge, in addition to school facilities, are part of the complex.

Try Kids on the Go, a drop-in affair that allows local and visiting children to meet each other. Games, crafts, cooking, out-trips and more keep kids interested. The community centre also offers one-day workshops for children, including Valentine's Day baking, puppetry, and candle making. Kids gymnastics classes, dance sessions, and karate lessons can also be arranged.

Meadow Park Arena

Six kilometres north of Whistler Village on Highway 99. Information Line: 938-3133.

The Meadow Park Arena, with its NHL-size ice surface and heated viewing lobby, opened in 1992. In addition to regular public ice skating, there are special parent and tot skates and teen skates. In January, a pizza and video night for teens starts with a skate. A free slice of pizza and free popcorn are included. A Valentine's Day parent and tot skate lets children dress up for a skate; a free hot chocolate and special Valentine's Day cookie are included. Kids Drop-in Hockey is occasionally offered. From April to August, in-line skating, roller hockey, and ball hockey sessions take over the rink. Skate rental and repair is available. Public skating schedules are subject to change. Contact the arena for times and programs.

Meadow Park Aquatic Centre

Located next to the Meadow Park Arena. Information Line: 938-3133.

This new aquatic centre includes a leisure pool with "beach access," a toddler pool, and active "river rapids" plus swim programs from toddlers to youth.

Christmas is for kids

The resort really shines for kids at Christmas. In mid-December, Delta Mountain Inn (932-7346) hosts a kid's gingerbread house workshop, assisted by its culinary Team Canada chefs. Children under 10 must be accompanied by an adult. Santa's Breakfast happens the Saturday before Christmas. Check with individual hotels for their Christmas programs and displays.

Concerts and carolling are featured throughout the resort, with guest appearances by the Whistler Singers and Whistler Children's Chorus. The valley's festive Christmas

Kids skiing

Ski schools provide instruction for both children and adults

FROM THE EXPERTS, here's a checklist for children heading for the slopes and skiing lessons:

Clothing must include long underwear and turtleneck, ski jacket and waterproof pants, warm hat, scarf, goggles or sunglasses, sunscreen and lip balm, warm socks, waterproof insulated mittens. Helmets are recommended and available to rent. Please tag and identify all articles of clothing and equipment.

Ensure that your child is well rested and has a good breakfast.

If your child is using his or her own equipment, please bring him or her dressed and ready to go.

Allow 30 minutes to sign your child up (additional time may be needed if rentals are required).

Tears are not uncommon. Instructors are trained to calm the fears of the child.

If you wish to check on your child, please telephone or watch from afar. Mid-day visits may bring back the tears.

Don't force your child into skiing. Children will learn when they're ready.

Street entertainers amuse children and adults

up snow slider does the trick at the base of Blackcomb Mountain, where families can toboggan at night under the lights. Blackcomb also puts on family nights during winter weekends. Sleigh rides, tobogganing, snowmobile rides, and hot chocolate are included. Smaller children enjoy tobogganing at Balsam Park, a small playground located off Lorimer Road at the intersection of Balsam Way and Easy Street.

Games and toys

Check out Great Games & Toys in Whistler's Marketplace (932-2043). To take your kids tobogganing, ask for their inexpensive roll-up snow slider.

Rodeo time

Mid-May is Lillooet Lake Rodeo time in Mount Currie, 6 kilometres north of Pemberton. Organized by local Native bands, the rodeo is a casual, colourful event. Follow Highway 99 from Mount Currie toward Lillooet to the Rodeo Grounds, approximately 6 kilometres along the gravel section of the highway. On Labour Day weekend, catch the Lillooet Lake Rodeo, also held at the Mount Currie Rodeo Grounds. Call the Spirit Circle Art, Craft & Tea Company (894-6336) for more

lights festival begins in late November and peaks over the Christmas season. Sleigh rides and tobogganing make the most of the season.

Family Christmas activities begin early in December at the Myrtle Philip Community Centre. Preschoolers share breakfast with Santa, bake unique holiday treats, and make holiday crafts. Older children bake and decorate their very own Christmas mansion, make fancy gift wrap, and join a week-long Christmas Break Day Camp. At the Meadow Park Arena, Holidays on Ice is a special event shared with the Whistler Skating Club. Children enjoy an old-fashioned Christmas skate with trees and lights, carolling, hot chocolate and goodies, plus a visit from Santa. Admission is a loonie ($1) and a donation to the Christmas food bank.

Whistler Wonderland

Located in the lower level of the Whistler Conference Centre. Telephone: 932-2422.

A family arcade with more than 70 video games, air hockey and pool tables, a nine-hole mini-golf course, children's play area, and comfortable eating area. Call ahead for hours of operation.

Movies

Take in a first-run movie at the 300-seat Dolby Surround Rainbow Theatre (932-2422); two showings nightly with weekend and rainy day matinees in the lower level of the Whistler Conference Centre. Or pick up a video from rental stores in Whistler Village, Whistler Creek, Nester's Square, and Whistler's Marketplace. For telephone numbers, see Children's Amenities on page 133.

Winter nights

Tobogganing is one sport that doesn't require a lot of training or special equipment. A roll-

information. Children 12 and under are free.

Books

Browse the Whistler Public Library (932-5564), located behind the Municipal Hall. Armchair Books (932-5557) also has a good selection of children's books.

Have llama, will travel

The best of companions on the trail, llamas are intelligent andsurefooted and don't complain when they carry your family's gear. Their padded feet and cleanliness on the trail make them the ideal travelling partners for environmentally conscious kids. Not to mention that they're lots of fun, too. Three- to five-day camping experiences in alpine settings, one-day family outings, or birthday celebrations are possible with Brackendale's Cloudraker Llamas (898-4249) or with Owl Creek Llama Treks, north of Mount Currie on the Pemberton Portage Road (894-6617). Call for more information.

Interpretive nature tours and walks

Blackcomb and Whistler mountain staff can advise you about walks best suited to your child's age and fitness level. During the summer season, children and youth under 15 ride free to the top of the mountains when accompanied by an adult; maximum five children per adult. Students (16–18 years) receive a discount on lift tickets.

Children should be properly dressed for a mountaintop visit. Sneakers, a warm jacket, or sweater, and sun hats or caps are standard gear. Always remember, the weather is changeable up

In-line skating takes advantage of the paved areas in Whistler

above.

Both mountains offer a variety of complimentary tours throughout the day; ranging from easy orientation walks to view the local flora and fauna, geology, and natural beauty to a challenging 1 to 1- to 1 1/2-hour walk through alpine meadows to the pristine beauty of Harmony Lake. Alpine wildflowers are in full bloom from mid-July through August.

Bikes, 'boards, and other wheels

Your kids can bring their own bicycles, skateboards, or in-line skates or rent from one of Whistler's many rental shops. The Valley Trail is an easy-going route for the above activities. See "Whistler in Summer" for rental information.

Adventure camps

For kids who want to windsurf, horseback ride, sail, rock climb, or barrel down a mountain on a bicycle, Tamwood International Camps (893-5566) is just the answer. From late June to early September, kids can take part in one-day to week-long sessions

of instruction. Activities also include arts and crafts, field games, glacier tours, nature hikes, in-line skating, and even snowboarding. The camp mixes education with good times, offering an English-as-a-second language component for children with English as a second language. Programs operate for children from 6 to 16 years of age.

Call Whistler Parks and Recreation (938-3133) for information on community-run day camps held for kids throughout the summer.

Nature watch

A free copy of the BC Parks booklet *Things to Do Outdoors* is available by writing to BC Parks, 1610 Mount Seymour Road, North Vancouver, BC V7G 1L3. Telephone: 929-4818. Designed for children, it shows them how to recognize animal tracks, identify swimming birds, and take a closer look at lichens, among other activities.

Living classroom

The gentle 3.2 kilometre hike into Cheakamus Lake is one of the most popular in the area. Before exploring the lake area, stop at the Whistler Interpretive Forest, 3.4 kilometres south of the Whistler Infocentre. Large, paneled information signs, interpretive sites, forestry demonstrations, and other educational features are located inside the working forest area.

The interpretive forest is a living classroom of 3500 hectares. Elevation rises from 600 metres to more than 1600 metres. Its geological history shows a mix of ancient seabeds, mountain uplifting, and recent volcanoes. Three biogeoclimatic zones are described for this region; most of the forest is in the Coastal Western Hemlock Zone, with the Mountain Hemlock and Subalpine Fir zones occuring at higher elevations.

Lawn sports

If you want to have a lot of fun and fresh air without too much effort, the Whistler Outdoor Experience Company (932-3389; Fax: 932-4469) rents equipment for lawn sports, such as croquet, horseshoes, boccè ball, badminton, volleyball, and tug-of-war.

The Hobbit House

Alpha Lake Park is home to the Hobbit House, a delightful children's playhouse designed by inventive architect and engineer Eric Scragg. An environmental scrounger, Scragg salvaged deformed cedar trees and transformed them into a building that children—and hobbits—love. The naturally curved hand and porch rails make the Hobbit House look as if it's just sprung out of the ground.

Beach action

Whistler's seven free parks and five local lakes can be en-

Kids' Kamp is a great way for kids to learn to ski and have fun

joyed in many ways. Picnic areas, beaches, playgrounds, and washrooms are located throughout the park system. The paved Valley Trail is great for walking, biking, or in-line skating.

Tennis pros

Many of Whistler Resort's hotels offer tennis lessons for children as well as adults. Additional courts, both public and private, are located throughout the valley. Some parks include free public courts. Call Whistler Parks and Recreation at 938-3133 for their locations.

Chateau Whistler (938-8000) runs its daily Tennis Tigers camps in July and Au-

gust. Classes are designed for young players, 5 to 12 years of age. Three tennis courts provide private and group lessons for older children and adults.

Families visiting the area

Child minding

A **SPECIAL PROGRAM** on Blackcomb Mountain babysits children 18 months to 3 years while parents ski. Crafts, circle time, outdoor play, and an afternoon rest period pace the activity. Pre-registration is required since enrolment is limited. Après-ski child minding for 4- to 14-year-olds is available from 3:30 pm to 5:30 pm.

regularly throughout the summer months may want to join the Whistler Valley Tennis Club on Lake Placid Road (938-3138). This community project, opened in 1988, has five courts. All-inclusive fees are $30 for juniors 13–17. Children under 12 play free with adult sign-up.

Cruisin' along

For a birthday celebration or just for fun, rent a gleaming, beautifully restored chauffeur-driven 1959 Cadillac Flattop or a 1955 Buick

Kids and water automatically hit it off at the old swimming hole

Special. Passengers are taken on a tour around Whistler's lakes, parks, golf courses, sports centres, historic locations, and notable residences. Tours leave every 90 minutes from Jimmy D's Roadhouse Restaurant (4005 Whistler Way), seven days a week from 9:00 am to 8:00 pm. Call 932-2259 to book.

Ski cool

Skiing is the original family activity in Whistler. Both mountains have a broad range of programs for kids of all ages. Whistler Mountains's Ski Scamps program provides lessons for some 17,000 young people a year, employing as many as 90 instructors during peak times. Blackcomb's Kids' Kamp ski school is the largest in Canada. Private lessons are also available.

For more information about ski lessons for your children, call Whistler Mountain at 932-3434 or Blackcomb Mountain at 938-7308 or 687-1032 from Vancouver.

Whistler Mountain

Whistler Mountain's Ski Scamps program caters to children from 2 years to 12 years of age. Special facilities and equipment are specifically designed for children. All instructors are trained to work with kids.

Programs are half or full days. They can include ski instruction, lunch, and indoor activities such as crafts and games. Classes are organized according to age and skiing ability. Participants meet at Whistler Creekside or Whistler Village.

Ski Scamps

Taught by specially trained in-

structors, children spend the day with a group of children learning proper ski techniques through games and group activities.

Personalities and abilities are assessed to make learning to ski fun. The program has three levels: Wee Scamps (2- to 4-year-olds), Snow Scamps (5- to 12-year-olds) and Mountain Scamps (up to 12 years old).

Wee Scamps

A low-key introduction to skiing for children from 2 to 4 years of age. One- to three-hour sessions combine arts and crafts, storytelling, and a rest period with ski classes.

Snow Scamps

Limited classes of 5 children from 5 to 12 years master snowplow turns and snowplow stops. Classes are approximately 3.5 hours long.

Mountain Scamps

Four-hour sessions take more advanced students up to 12 years of age onto more challenging hills. Lessons are limited to eight students, grouped according to age and ability.

Club Free youth programs

Club Free, for young people 12 to 16 years of age, offers separate snowboarding and skiing classes. Club Freeski participants spend the day with a training coach exploring powder, bumps, gates, and steeps. Club Freeride's top snowboarding pros improve skills on the mountain's best boarding locations.

All-day lessons in either skiing or snowboarding give young people a chance to develop skills, meet new friends, and attend special events.

Blackcomb Mountain

Blackcomb is committed to developing young skiers. In addition to lessons, special kids' menus and free skiing for children six and under are offered on the mountain.

Kids' Kamp

An important step for children is a first set of skis and a chance to explore the thrill of speed and the power of control. Kids progress quickly from stopping and snowplowing to stem turns. Games keep learning fun. The children's program is well planned and includes specially selected instructors as well as special on-mountain terrain gardens to help kids hone specific skills.

Wee Wizards

Children as young as 2 years old can begin skiing if they're so inclined. Wee Wizards on Blackcomb Mountain teaches the fundamentals in a caring environment. Pre-registration is required, since enrolment is limited.

Super Kids

Four- to 12-year-olds enjoy programs tailored to their individual abilities. Daily progress cards show how far they have advanced.

Mini Masters

Led by Blackcomb's best instructors, Mini Masters is designed for 7- to 10-year-olds to gain skills for skiing powder and bumps and for cruising runs while exploring new trails.

Super Stars

A program designed for talented young 10- to 13-year-old skiers ready for black zones and extreme terrain.

Team Devo (Team Development)

Created for intermediate and advanced skiers and snowboarders, 13- to 16-year-old, who have developed beyond Kids' Kamp. Through high-level coaching in racing skills, young skiers master a variety of terrain and snow conditions, tackling legends like the Saudan Couloir, Pakalolo, and Ruby Bowl when they're ready. Instruction includes racing, moguls, steeps, ballet skiing, and freestyle.

Art outreach

Children and creativity are synonymous. Although sports are big time in the Whistler area, the arts are not neglected. Crafts, drawing, painting, piano, and live theatre all enjoy lively attention.

Art awareness

Each June, the Whistler Children's Art Festival spotlights young people's artwork throughout the resort. Call the Whistler Activity and Information Centre for details (932-2394). In addition to regular arts and crafts classes, the

Myrtle Philip Community Centre runs two-day art courses, such as Drawing and Painting for Young People. Call 938-7275.

Piano prodigies

Every July, the Young Artists' Experience provides 12 of Canada's most gifted pianists, aged 12 to 18 years, with an intensive two-week summer residency under the guidance of internationally acclaimed instructors. Young musicians explore classical music in master classes and festival concerts.

Since it was launched, the program has grown in popularity. It attracts students from across Canada, with a waiting list for entry. Modeled after the famous Aspen and Tanglewood summer music festivals, the program includes informal recitals held in the Rainbow Theatre for Whistler residents and visitors.

All hands on stage

Whistler Summer Theatre (986-4601) was established in 1991. From mid-July to mid-August, it runs two plays, one for children and one for family entertainment, in a 200-seat tent at the base of Blackcomb Mountain next to the Chateau Whistler Hotel. An afternoon children's performance, based on a classical story like Pinocchio, and a musical comedy are usually on the agenda. Children's theatre is presented daily at 4:00 pm (except Sundays). Adult shows (also suitable for older children) are shown daily at 8:00 pm (except Sundays).

Summer ski lessons

HORTSMAN GLACIER awaits youngsters during Blackcomb Mountain's summer skiing session, mid-June to August.

The Atomic Dave Murray Summer Ski Camp, operating since 1966, offers lessons for all ages and levels of skiers. As with other summer ski camps, activities are not limited to skiing. Mountain biking, volleyball, windsurfing, and in-line skating may also come with the package.

Camp Ride's six-day camps for snowboarders 12 years and up is taught by champion coaches.

For more information, call Blackcomb Mountain at 938-7308.

Children's amenities

Arcades
- Whistler Wonderland Mini-Golf: 932-2422

Fast food and family dining
- A&W Restaurant: 938-9165
- Boston Pizza: 932-7070
- Dusty's: 932-5543
- Hoz's Cafe: 932-4424
- Louie's Submarine: 932-9777
- McDonald's: 932-2813
- Misty Mountain Pizza Company: 932-2825
- Mondo Pizza: 938-9554
- Monk's Grill: 932-9677
- The Original Ristorante: 932-6408
- Peter's Underground: 932-4811
- Pika's: (Whistler Mountain) 932-3434
- Rendezvous (Blackcomb Mountain): 932-3775
- Settebello's: 932-3000
- Subway: 932-3244

Babysitters
- Blackcomb Mountain Kids' Kamp: 938-7308
- Sonja's Babysitting Service: 938-1498
- TLC Daycare (weekends and holidays): 932-5311
- Dandylion Daycare (7 days/week): 932-1119

Bakers
- Bakers Cottage: 932-2253
- Evergreens Bakery: 932-1982
- Husky Store & Deli: 932-3959
- Little Mountain Bakery: 932-4220
- Whistler Cookie Company: 932-2962

Books & games
- Armchair Books: 932-5577
- Great Games & Toys: 932-2043

Candy shops
- Going Nuts: 932-4676
- Rocky Mountain Chocolate Factory: 932-4100

Photo finishing
- Whistler 1 Hour Photo: 932-6612/932-6676
- Slalom (1 HR) Photo: 938-9090

Pharmacy
- Pharmasave: 932-2303/932-4251

Video services
Capture your vacation on film through one of the following video/photography companies.
- Long Run Video Productions: 932-4732
- Mountain Sharpshooters: 938-9100

Video rentals
- Boyd's: 932-6844. Video tapes and equipment rentals.
- Whistler Video: 932-3540. Video tapes and equipment rentals.
- Whistler's Other Video Store: 932-3980. Video tapes only.
- Wilderness Videos: 938-9793.
- McKeever's General Store: 932-3600. Video tapes only.

Northern Sea to Sky Highway

The Lillooet Rodeo adds a western touch to the mountains

At one time, few travellers ventured north along Highway 99 past Pemberton, 35 kilometres beyond Whistler. The route to Lillooet, 100 kilometres from Pemberton along the Duffey Lake Road, was strictly gravel, one step up from a logging road. Most chose the alternate

Trans-Canada Highway 1 to the Cariboo-Chilcotin/Lillooet region.

All this changed in 1992, when the route was upgraded to an extension of Highway 99. With the exception of a 9-kilometre gravel stretch through the Mount Currie Indian Reserve, the joys of pavement now entice a growing number of visitors to this once very isolated area. Another recently paved road leads through Mount Currie to D'Arcy and

Anderson Lake, a camping and boating area.

Travellers who like to get away from it all will appreciate the remoteness of the area. From Mount Currie to Lillooet, there's not a gas station in sight. Outhouses are located at the new Duffey Lake Provincial Park, the Joffre Lakes Recreation Area, and six BC Forest Service (BCFS) recreation sites along the way, but that's basically it for amenities. Past Mount Currie, a gravel turnoff

to Lillooet Lake leads to five more BCFS campsites, as well as several rustic resorts with cabins dotting the lake.

The lure is BC's backcountry and a route that traverses two climatic zones. Leaving the Coast Mountains, you travel into swooping semiarid valleys as you head to cowboy country, the Cariboo-Chilcotin region. Enroute are three double-backed switchbacks, waterfalls, fishing streams, and animals in the wild. For free detailed maps of the area, call or write the Squamish Forest District, 42000 Loggers Lane, Squamish, BC V0N 3G0, telephone: 898-2100; and the BC Ministry of Forests, Lillooet Forest District, Bag Service 700, Lillooet, BC V0K 1V0, telephone: 256-7631.

Duffey Lake Road (Highway 99)

The Romans have gone down in history as great road builders. Surely even they would be amazed at the tenacity of BC's early engineers and the Chinese labourers who tackled

Rocky Mountain bighorn ram

The Coast Mountain Circle Tour

ONCE CALLED THE Nugget Route, the Coast Mountain Circle Tour is 600 kilometres long, ideal for a leisurely two or three days of travel. Drive it clockwise or counterclockwise.

Day 1: Leave Whistler and travel north to Pemberton and Mount Currie. Pemberton Valley is ringed by a steep-walled alpine setting. From Mount Currie, try a side trip to D'Arcy, 42 kilometres away. See adult sockeye salmon at the Birkenhead Fish Hatchery, mid-August to mid-September. Follow Highway 99 to Lillooet (population 1800), located at Mile 0 of the Cariboo Wagon Road. It's rich in history, as the Lillooet Museum and Infocentre

on Main Street attests.

Day 2: From Lillooet, take a 109 kilometre side trip to Gold Bridge and local ghost towns. Or continue on Highway 99 to the historic Gold Rush junction town of Cache Creek. Ten kilometres directly south, Ashcroft is also known for its Old West aura and excellent fishing. Eighty kilometres south, where the Fraser and Thompson rivers meet, Lytton is a base for river rafters and rockhounds. From Lytton, the Trans-Canada Highway 1 follows the steep, scenic Fraser Canyon. Gold was discovered here in the late 1850s. Hope is the gateway (or back door) to the mighty Fraser River Canyon, which has

numerous local attractions, recreational lakes, and hiking and picnicking areas.

Day 3: Stay overnight at Hope or nearby Harrison Hot Springs, 28 kilometres away. Known for its mineral hot springs, the lakeside resort includes a public pool, boating, hiking, accommodations, and full amenities. Sasquatch Provincial Park, beyond Harrison, offers quiet lakes for fishing. Continue on to complete the tour in Vancouver.

For more information on the Coast Mountain Circle Tour, its accommodations, and its attractions, call 1-800-663-6000.

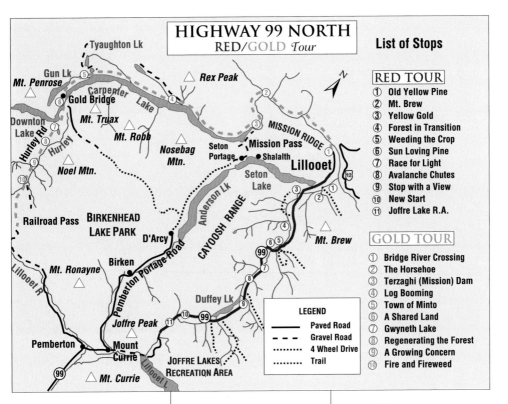

HIGHWAY 99 NORTH
RED/GOLD Tour

List of Stops

RED TOUR
1. Old Yellow Pine
2. Mt. Brew
3. Yellow Gold
4. Forest in Transition
5. Weeding the Crop
6. Sun Loving Pine
7. Race for Light
8. Avalanche Chutes
9. Stop with a View
10. New Start
11. Joffre Lake R.A.

GOLD TOUR
1. Bridge River Crossing
2. The Horsehoe
3. Terzaghi (Mission) Dam
4. Log Booming
5. Town of Minto
6. A Shared Land
7. Gwyneth Lake
8. Regenerating the Forest
9. A Growing Concern
10. Fire and Fireweed

LEGEND
— Paved Road
- - - Gravel Road
········· 4 Wheel Drive
········ Trail

daunting wilderness to open up areas for miners and settlers. Many thousands gave their lives in the process. Duffey Lake was named for Pvt. Sapper James Duffey of the Royal Engineers, one of the victims of early development. Sent out by Governor James Douglas to survey the area, Sapper Duffey froze to death on the Gold Rush Trail in 1861.

The Duffey Lake Road, now Highway 99, passes from the Coast Mountains into the Cayoosh Range along narrow Duffey Lake and even narrower canyons. It finally breaks free in semiarid ranchland on the banks of the Fraser River.

In 1975, the 85-kilometre Duffey Lake route was upgraded to a public road. Actual use, other than by logging companies, was minimal. Its transformation to a paved highway in 1991, at a cost of more than $22 million, has increased traffic. Nevertheless, the area has retained its isolation. Don't look for a gas station or restaurant enroute; there aren't any between Mount Currie and Lillooet.

The Duffey Lake (Cayoosh) Pass through the Coast Mountains is over 1300 metres high. The descent into Lillooet at 230 metres above sea level is spectacular. Snow conditions can be expected from the late fall well into spring. Watch for avalanche warning signs and instructions. Drive carefully, because logging trucks and motorcyclists are frequently in evidence.

Stopping over

Campers or picnickers will find a series of campsites, picnic tables, and outhouses along the route. In addition to the new Duffey Lake Provincial Park, visitors can stay overnight at six well-marked creekside recreation sites. Before reaching the west end of Duffey Lake, RVs can park in a flat area that was once a gravel pit.

The Joffre Lakes Recreation Area is also used for backcountry camping and hiking. A 10-minute trail leads to Lower Joffre Lake, one of three turquoise subalpine lakes. A trail to Middle and Upper Joffre lakes is a six-hour return trip with a gain in elevation of 400 metres. Joffre Lakes is a wilderness area at the

Pemberton's log museum is a reminder of pioneer days

northern extremity of the Cascade Mountains. Only experienced mountaineers should attempt mountain climbing or venture onto glaciers and snowfields. Be well prepared, equipped, and informed, before tackling its inner reaches.

The Red/Gold Tour

For unique insights into the Sea to Sky's northern areas, take the self-guided BC Ministry of Forests' Red and Gold forestry tours. Both tours begin at the Lillooet Museum and Infocentre. Head south through Lillooet toward Pemberton for the Red Tour. For the Gold Tour, head north from Lillooet for 1.5 kilometres, then turn left before the Old Mill Plaza onto Moha Road.

For complete tour information, call or write the BC Ministry of Forests, Lillooet Forest District, Bag Service 700, Lillooet, BC V0K 1V0,

telephone 256-7631

A. Gold Tour

1) Bridge River Crossing, kilometre 7.5

The mouth of the Bridge River is named Xwisten by local Native people, meaning "place of foam." Nearby are traditional Native fishing grounds. On the bench above the bridge (to the north) is an old Native village and cemetery.

2) The Horseshoe, kilometre 30.4

In 1932, Lower Bridge River Placer Ltd. began operations on the north bank of the Bridge River. It planned to remove gravel using a high-pressure hose, exposing gold-rich layers below. The gravel proved too deep and the operation failed. A ramp used to stage a spectacular truck crash in the 1978 French movie *The Threat*, starring Yves Montand, can still be seen.

3) Terzaghi (Mission) Dam, kilometre 49.4

The Bridge River Power Project, begun in 1948, was completed in 1960. The dam is 56 metres high and holds back one million cubic metres of water.

4) Log Booming, kilometre 77

Across the lake at Tommy Creek, logging took place in the late 1970s. The logs were brought across the water in booms and loaded on trucks. Some logs were milled at a small sawmill located near Jones Creek at 70.8 kilometres. In the early 1980s, tree planters used boats to gain access to the logged area in order to plant the site with Douglas-fir seedlings.

5) Town of Minto, kilometre 97.6

Under Carpenter Lake lies the town of Minto. Built by the Minto Gold Company, it was finished in 1934, complete with streets, water, hotel, store, mine buildings, and electricity. The town was abandoned to make way for the Carpenter Lake Reservoir.

6) A Shared Land, kilometre 106.1

The desire for gold resulted in the mining towns of Gold Bridge and Bralorne. This activity helped create access for future logging. The many roads in the area have in turn given recreationists access to fishing, hiking, snowmobiling, and skiing areas.

7) Gwyneth Lake, kilometre 114.3

In 1979, the mountain pine beetle population near Gwyneth Lake increased dramatically. Mild winters, warm summers, and a uniform stand of trees were leading to an infestation of epidemic proportions. To control the spread of the fungus-carrying beetle and minimize loss of timber value, 360 hectares were clearcut.

8) Regenerating the Forest, kilometre 115.6

This clearcut contains three examples of site preparation. Site preparation is a silvicultural activity designed to improve conditions for the planting, survival, and growth of seedlings. On 150 hectares, enough pine cones covered the area to ensure natural regeneration for reforestation. On 170 hectares, the debris left after logging was piled by machine to reduce fire hazard and remove obstructions to planting. On 3.5 hectares of wet ground, mounds were made using an excavator to provide more favourable growing conditions for planted pine and spruce seedlings.

Horseback riding is a cherished pursuit in the area, with several outfitters available for treks

9) A Growing Concern, kilometre 128.8

In the late 1970s, logging extended to higher elevations in the Hurley River Valley. These sites have high snow levels and short growing seasons. Research trials were established at this location in 1985 to assess the timing of replanting and the effect that extreme climatic conditions have on seedling growth and survival.

10) Fire and Fireweed, kilometre 132.6

Across the valley is a large burned area that originated mainly from a wildfire in 1976. This location, with its converging valleys, is the target of thunder and lightning storms. Lightning has caused the area to be burned a number of times.

B. Red Tour

1) Old Yellow Pine

This majestic tree is commonly known as yellow or ponderosa pine. It shares the warm dry valley bottoms with Douglas-fir.

2) Mt. Brew's Gold Nuggets, kilometre 7.5

Across the deep canyon of Cayoosh Creek on the middle slopes of Mt. Brew, two logged areas are visible. These north-facing slopes have deep, rich soils and are valuable as habitat as well as for the production of timber crops. A logging road was built up the slope from Cayoosh Creek in 1977 to allow cutting of Douglas-fir, many of which were infested with western spruce budworm.

3) Yellow Gold and Green Gold, kilometre 15.3

Chinese placer miners worked the creek banks along this section of Cayoosh Creek from 1887 to 1889. In 1895, Arthur Noel and Joe Copeland discovered a gold vein 515 metres above the creek. In 1980, the mountain walls were scaled with bulldozer crawler tractors, rock drills, and explosives to build a logging road on Seton Ridge. The road now provides access to a hiking trail to alpine meadows.

4) Forest in Transition, kilometre 23.4

This is the halfway point between the hot, dry forests of the Fraser River and the cool, wet forests around Duffey Lake. Stop at the Cottonwood

Pemberton/Mount Currie amenities

Transportation
- Air BC: 688-5515 (Vancouver)
- Alliance Taxi and Limousine: 894-6565
- Maverick Coach Lines: 255-1171 (Vancouver)
- Pemberton Airport: 894-6761
- BC Rail: 984-5246 (Vancouver)

Emergency
- Ambulance Service: BC 894-6353
- BC Automobile Association Emergency Service: 1-800-663-2222
- Forest Fires: Call operator and ask for Zenith 5555
- RCMP/Police Emergency: 894-6126
- Pemberton Health Centre: 894-6633
- Stl'atl'imx Nation Tribal Police: 894-6124

Non-emergency
- Big Ozzie Mountain Pharmacy: 894-6707
- BC Forest Service: 894-6112
- Highway Information: 1-800-663-4997
- Mount Currie Indian Band: 894-6115
- Mount Currie Post Office: 894-6241
- Off-Road Auto Body and Towing (24 Hour): 894-6767
- Pemberton Health Centre: 894-6633. Outpatient/emergency service only.
- Pemberton Sportsmen's Wildlife Association: 894-6028
- Pemberton and District Chamber of Commerce: 894-6175
- Village of Pemberton: 894-6135

Accommodations
- Chris's Corner Bed & Breakfast: 894-6787
- Mount Currie Bed & Breakfast: 894-6864
- Hitching Post Motel (Mount Currie): 894-6276
- Lillooet Lake Lodge, by operator: Radio Pemberton 1YR, Channel H625672
- Pemberton Creekside Bed & Breakfast: 894-6520
- Pemberton Hollow Bed & Breakfast: 894-6410
- Pemberton Hotel: 894-6313

Groceries & gas
- Mountain View Esso: 894-6220
- Mount Currie Grocery and Gas: 894-6320
- Pemberton General Store: 894-6233
- Petro-Canada Quik-Mart & Gas Bar: 894-5388
- Pioneer Market: 894-6345

Outdoor markets
- Mount Currie Gathered From the Earth Market: 894-6336
- Pemberton Valley Farmer's Market: 894-5558

Recreation
- Adventures on Horseback: 894-6968/894-6155
- Lillooet Jetboating: 938-0411
- McLeod Creek Wilderness Ranch: 894-5704
- Pemberton Adventure Ranch: 894-6601/toll-free in BC 1-800-303-2628
- Pemberton Helicopter Tours: 894-6919
- Pemberton Soaring: 894-5727
- Pemberton Stables: 894-6615
- Pemberton Golf & Country Club: 894-5122
- WD Bar Ranch Lil'Wat Adventures: 894-5669
- The Whistler Outdoor Experience Company: 932-3389
- Whistler Jet-Boating Ltd.: 894-5200
- Whistler River Jet: 932-3389

Other
- Sea to Sky Books: 894-6833
- Pemberton Museum: 894-6135
- Pemberton Post Office: 894-6816
- Pemberton Valley News: 894-6610
- Lillooet Lake Herbs and Flowers: 894-6508
- Salix Farms Herbs and Flowers: 894-5558

Special Days

February
- Spud Valley Annual Loppet (Cross-country ski meet)

May
- Birkenhead Lake & Blackwater Lake Fishing Derby
- Lillooet Lake Rodeo at Mount Currie Rodeo Grounds

June
- Pemberton Frontier Days
- D'Arcy's 4X4 Rally and Salmon Barbecue
- Voyageur Challenge Canoe Race, Lillooet River
- Annual Pemberton Airport Pancake Breakfast
- Canada Week Festival

July
- Canada Day Celebrations
- Anderson Lake Salmon Barbecue
- Annual Great Lillooet River Barrel Race

September
- Lillooet Lake Rodeo at Mount Currie Rodeo Grounds
- Pemberton Chamber of Commerce Golf Tournament

December
- Mount Currie Craft Fair with Native artisans

Recreation Site to enjoy the view.

5) Weeding the Crop, kilometre 29.5

In order for a forest site to have maximum timber production, trees need to be thinned, spaced, and "weeded." This cutblock was treated with herbicides, beginning in 1987, as a method of controlling the growth of deciduous trees, which initially grow faster than conifers, use up soil nutrients, and block the light for the slower-growing trees. Today the BC Forest Service uses much fewer chemical or herbicide controls for this purpose.

6) Sun-Loving Pine, kilometre 30.1

Lodgepole pine requires a lot of sunlight. It grows poorly in the shade of other plants. This cutblock was planted with lodgepole pine in 1980, but other plants—referred to as "brush"—grew quickly and began to shade out the trees. In 1982 and 1984, the brush was cut manually.

7) Race for Light, kilometre 37.3

This stand of lodgepole pine, naturally seeded, has grown since a forest fire in 1958. Note that many of the trees are densely packed. The competition for light, water, and nutrients is so intense that the trees are spindly.

8) Avalanche Chutes, kilometre 42.6

Across Cayoosh Creek there is a steep avalanche pathway down the mountain, with its boundaries marked by deciduous brush. Heavy snowfalls,

A gathering at the Mount Currie Rustic Campground

changing weather, and steep terrain contribute to unstable snowpack, which can result in avalanches.

9) Stop with a View, kilometre 47.2

You are now at the new Duffey Lake Provincial Park which has 48 rustic campsites located mostly on back country roads. A spectacular view of glaciated peaks can be seen to the southwest.

10) New Start, kilometre 66.8

This area was logged in 1972, control-burned in 1974, then planted with spruce in 1978. Walk through the plantation for a closer look. It is classified as satisfactorily stocked, but it may need future thinning and fertilization.

11) Joffre Lakes Recreation Area, kilometre 69.3

This recreation area was developed in 1973. Some 2000 people visit annually for hiking, camping, fishing, hunting, and cross-country skiing. A round-trip (11-kilometre) trail takes up to six hours to hike.

Pemberton and valley

Pemberton (population 700), "the little town at the foot of the mountain," is a 30-minute drive north from Whistler. Set in the broad, flat Pemberton Valley at the base of Mt. Currie,

Forest rules for safe use

LITTER IS UNSIGHTLY for people following you and can be dangerous to wildlife. Take your litter with you.

Fire is one of the forest's worst enemies. Use your car ashtray, light campfires in safe places, and make sure they're completely out when you finish with them. If you discover a fire that you can't put out yourself, call Zenith 5555 and report it immediately.

Remember you share the highways and Forest Service roads with industrial vehicles. All regular highway rules also apply. Give way to industrial traffic. Use your headlights.

Meager Creek Hot Springs

GETTING TO MEAGER Creek Hot Springs isn't the easiest trip in the world. In some places, where the backcountry logging road narrows to little more than a trail on the edge of a rocky mountainside, it's even downright scary.

Which may explain the lure of this out-of-the-way hot springs, 45 kilometres northwest of Pemberton village. It's hard to get to, isolated, and something of a legend. Tales of all-night parties, summer and winter, abound. During the day, however, the springs can be fairly quiet.

Meager Creek's remoteness lures summer and winter bathers

What makes the springs in Meager Creek so hot—52° to 100°C—is geothermal energy. Experts describe the creek's geothermal area as the most significant energy discovery in Canada. Nine volcanoes, part of the Garibaldi Group, form the Meager Creek volcanic complex. If developed, Meager Mountain could provide enough thermal energy to power an entire city. A geothermal plant is proposed for a site 7 kilometres from the hot springs on the opposite side of a mountain ridge.

In 1984, heavy rains swept massive amounts of debris off clearcut slopes into Meager Creek and the Lillooet River. Visitors to

the hot springs were helicoptered out; it was a year before the area was reopened. A group of local volunteers, Friends of Meager Creek Hot Springs, dedicated themselves to rehabilitating the Forest Service recreation site, hot pools, and trails. Their handiwork shaped two public hot tubs (one cooler, the other hotter) along the sandy riverbank, plus a sauna.

To get to Meager Creek Hot Springs, follow the paved Pemberton Meadows Road through the picturesque, tranquil farmlands. At the 28-kilometre point, the pavement ends. Turn right at the Coast Mountain Outdoor School turnoff, crossing over the Lillooet River bridge. Continue on the gravel

road that follows along the Lillooet River. At Mile 24 marker, turn left and continue a few kilometres beyond, watching for a sign at the parking lot.

The roads are best June to September. In winter, you will have to take chains and ski in part of the way. Avoid the area in spring and fall, when heavy rains can make the roads treacherous. Be on the alert for logging trucks.

For more information on Meager Creek Hot Springs, call the Forest Service recreation site (campsites and outhouses), or call or write the Squamish Forest District, 42000 Loggers Lane, Squamish, BC V0N 3G0, telephone 898-2100.

Frankie Jim, Mount Currie bow maker

FORM AND FUNCTION work together when Frankie Jim of Mount Currie makes a bow and arrow. "Bows were one of our traditional tools," he says of the skill he is helping to keep alive in the Lil'wat area.

The Mount Currie man was taught bowmaking by his father at the age of eight. "My father

Frankie Jim

was very patient, even though at first my bows just kept breaking."

Since then, Frankie Jim, now a constable with the Stl'atl'imx Nation Tribal Police and a member of the Mount Currie Band Council, has made hundreds of bows and arrows, a few of which he sells. Most, however, are destined for the local community, a way to carry on tradition.

it's the ideal centre for farming and ranching.

The town was named for Joseph Despard Pemberton, a colonial surveyor appointed by Governor James Douglas of the Vancouver Colony. Originally built at the north end of Lillooet Lake in 1859, Pemberton was strategically located on a main transportation route to the Cariboo gold fields. From the spring of 1858 onward, thousands of prospectors followed this route north to the gold fields rather than risk death on the precipitous Fraser Canyon route. Pemberton's heyday ended swiftly with the opening of the Cariboo Road through the Fraser Canyon in 1864.

A local group is now trying to re-establish the original townsite as a tourist attraction. To have a look, drive along the Mount Currie gravel section of Highway 99 to the point where pavement begins again. On your left is a little road that climbs up the side of a hill. A walk of under 2 kilometres takes you to the original 2-hectare site.

With the extension of Highway 99 to Lillooet, Pemberton's wide open vistas and small-town charm are attracting an increasing number of visitors. In the process, tourism facilities have been expanded, starting with the Pemberton Infocentre (894-6175), located on Highway 99 just before the turnoff into the town. Although logging is still in evidence, cafés and coffeehouses, art galleries, and bed and breakfast stops have popped up enroute.

Winter or summer, recreation opportunities are plenty and varied. Stay in the valley or head into the backcountry for alpine hiking, climbing, heli-skiing, cross-country skiing, boating, hang-gliding, rodeos, alpine lakes, river rafting, kayaking, hunting, fishing, wildlife viewing, hot springs, and arts and crafts. Outdoor activities of all types are run by locally based companies. See page 140 for listings and for Pemberton amenities and special days.

Mount Currie

The small village of Mount Currie (population 1400) is more than immediately meets the eye. Many of the 1000-strong Interior Salish Stl'atl'imx (pronounced stat-lee-am) Nation Indian band who reside on the reserve here live in a residential subdivision at the northwest end of Lillooet Lake. The Xitolacw townsite turnoff is approximately 5 kilometres along the gravel stretch of Highway 99 (known locally as the Lillooet Lake Road), followed by another 4 kilometres along a second gravel road. The site, once a turnip farm, is now a full-fledged, if isolated, community. A new community centre adjacent to a large playing field hosts low-key annual gatherings, such as Lil'wat Days. Visitors are welcome at these events. Telephone the Mount Currie Indian Band office at 894-6115 for more information.

Not everyone from the Mount Currie reserve moved to the new community. Some remain in the 100-year-old village, the centre of which is located at the junction of Highway 99 and the Portage Road to D'Arcy. Mount Currie was named after John Currie, a Scottish settler who lived here in the 1860s with his

Spud Valley

LEAVE YOUR POTATOES at home when you head for Pemberton. Known affectionately as Spud Valley, the Pemberton Meadows area is famous for its virus-free potato farms. In 1949, the Pemberton Seed Control Area was established, making it illegal to bring potatoes into the region.

Some 200 hectares in the valley produce a yield of about 28 tonnes per hectare—on average 40,320 plants per hectare.

Hemmed in by mountain ranges, the physically isolated valley protects farms from virus-carrying aphids. Keeping the spuds pure is the job of the Pemberton Valley Seed Growers, which tests plantlets on their way to the fields for known diseases and viruses. Only Pemberton seeds can be grown here. New varieties are okayed by the University of British Columbia and are repeatedly tested before they're planted.

Pemberton potatoes get around. Through UBC, samples of Pemberton spuds are requested by all the potato-growing provinces in Canada and the potato-growing states in the US. Samples are sent to China, Saudi Arabia, Scotland, South Korea, Sri Lanka, Peru, South Africa, and former Eastern Bloc countries. Its reputation for perfect produce has made Pemberton the seed potato capital of North America.

Native wife. The local name for the valley is Lil'wat, one translation of which is "the fir tree" in the Stl'atl'imx language.

Mt. Currie, a massive 2590 metres high, is regarded as a sacred mountain by the Lil'wat people. Local carvers now reproduce modern versions of ancient stone images found in the area, including the famous Mount Currie owl. Their work can be seen in the Spirit Circle Art, Craft & Tea Company.

Another long tradition in Mount Currie is its rodeo. Lil'wat people have a history of riding and racing. During the winter, horseback races were once held by Native competitors down the main street of the village, with women as well as men famed for their racing abilities. The twice-yearly Lillooet Lake Rodeo is held over the Victoria Day and Labour Day weekends in May and September.

Mount Currie is growing slowly. A bed and breakfast accommodation, a motel, a coffeehouse/art gallery, and a restaurant are now located here. Gas up if required, since the next gas station along Highway 99 is in Lillooet, 94 kilometres away. (Note: the Mount Currie station is not open 24 hours.)

The Harrison-Lillooet Wagon Trail

The Duffey Lake trail was, in fact, not the first route northward. As you head toward Lillooet past Mount Currie, you'll cross a bridge over Lillooet Lake. Shortly after, a right-hand turn leads down a

Free-range horses are frequently found in this area

gravel road along the lake. This was the original Harrison-Lillooet route—also called the Douglas Trail—an expensive and lengthy passage through difficult terrain.

The route, from Harrison Lake to the north end of Lillooet Lake, was first surveyed in 1846-1847 by Alexander Caulfield Anderson. The Harrison-Lillooet Wagon Trail consisted of 240 rugged kilometres. After 1858, the journey was largely undertaken by miners desperate to get to the Cariboo gold fields.

Travellers from Harrison Lake to Lillooet Lake took four sternwheelers enroute. Portages from the north end of Harrison Lake to Lillooet Lake and along the road from Port Pemberton to Anderson

Attention hikers and mountaineers

BEFORE EMBARKING on any trip into the backcountry, register with the local Royal Canadian Mounted Police (RCMP). During working hours, visit the Pemberton RCMP Detachment located on Prospect Street, near the Forest Service Office (emergency telephone: 894-6126; non-emergency 894-6634) or evenings at the front desk of the Pemberton Hotel (894-6313). All information on the forms is strictly confidential and is used only if emergency help or evacuation is required. Those who don't register may be billed for any rescue services required on their behalf.

Motorists must be cautious in winter and early spring. Watch

Only experienced mountaineers should tackle the Joffre Lakes Recreation Area

for avalanche warning signs. Do not stop in avalanche areas.

Lake were arduous treks. A rail car pulled by a winch carried miners from Anderson Lake to Seton Lake on a short portage of 183 metres.

In 1860, construction began on a more direct road through the Fraser Canyon to the gold fields beyond Lillooet. With completion of the Fraser route in 1864, the Harrison-Lillooet trail was largely forgotten. It can still be retraced by land using provincial, BC Hydro, and Forest Service roads. Five recreation sites are available for picnicking and camping along Lillooet Lake. Travellers must watch for active logging.

Highlights on the Lillooet Lake Road include several rustic resorts, the St. Agnes Well hot springs, and Skookumchuck, a remote Native village. Prominent spires distinguish Skookumchuck's Roman Catholic Church of the Holy Cross, built in 1905. At the turn of the century, Skookumchuck was the gathering place for the Native people of the Harrison-Pemberton area.

Recreation maps are available from the Squamish Forest District, 42000 Loggers Lane, Squamish, BC V0N 3G0, telephone 898-2100; and the Lillooet Forest District, 650 Industrial Place, Bag Service 700, Lillooet, BC V0K 1V0, telephone 256-1200.

Spirit Circle Art, Craft & Tea Company

A COFFEEHOUSE with a difference. the Spirit Circle Art, Craft & Tea Company is a unique coffeehouse/art gallery. A stream flows through the back yard, where a teepee with a brass bed makes an unusual overnight accommodation. Bears sometimes visit the spot where owner Deanna Pilling grows fresh vegetables for her customers. Visitors can drop in, browse, and buy from a wide selection of Native arts and crafts and chat with local Lil'wat people. Light meals, including hot bannock (a Native bread) with butter and honey, fresh salads, and coffee to rival the best are served here. Swamp tea and *xusum* (pronounced hoshum), a cold drink made with soapberries, are both recommended. All produce is organically grown. "The focus and the vision of the Spirit Circle is to foster ecological and cultural biodiversity," says Deanna, who opened the coffeehouse in 1992 after falling in love with the area.

With the help of the Native community of Mount Currie, Deanna sells and serves wild-

On the Circle's patio, a skull is bleached by the sun

grown and garden-grown teas. Swamp tea is such a favourite that gatherers have been known to dig underneath a metre or more of snow to collect a few kilograms.

Handmade crafts from the community decorate the airy restaurant. Renowned Interior Salish bark and cedar root baskets are interspersed with stone and wood carvings, beadwork, and a selection of books and greeting cards. Outside, a model of an *eshken*, an aboriginal pithouse indigenous to the area, is

being dug as a display.

In the summer, Deanna organizes a weekly farmers' market and ice cream shop. Some of her produce comes from the Stl'atl'imx Producers, a group of Native certified organic growers. The Gathered From the Earth Market sells fruit and vegetables, eggs, jams, and locally made crafts.

The Spirit Circle Art, Craft & Tea Company is located in Mount Currie on Highway 99. For more information, call 894-6336.

Preserving the forests

AS MANY AS 94,000 people in BC make their living in the forest industry. Another 140,000 to 184,000 people (depending on who is counting, the government or the forestry industry) are indirectly employed.

Forestry was one of the earliest industries in BC. In the beginning, it was inconceivable that the vast old-growth stands would ever be depleted. More than 100 years of activity, and the introduction of modern technologies that make it possible to remove timber from precipitous mountainsides, has proved this assumption wrong. Both those who make their livelihood from logging and those who want to protect the forests that remain are struggling to find solutions.

The Squamish-Lillooet forestry areas have experienced their share of turmoil in recent years. Clearcutting of old growth forests, Native burial sites, and traditional food gathering areas, destruction of spotted-owl habitat, the intrusion of logging roads into remote areas, roadblocks, and destruction of forest industry property have lead to demonstrations and distress on both sides.

In the hope of sustaining and renewing its forests, the Province of British Columbia instituted a new Forest Practices Code, with new definitions of rules and regulations, in the spring of 1994. Companies now face fines of up to $1 million for transgressions against the code, which will be fully in effect by 1996.

A forest renewal plan was also introduced in April 1994. Some $400 million annually from stumpage fees and royalties is

Logging practices are facing changes in order to replenish and protect BC's wilderness (inset: a BC clearcut)

now earmarked for forest renewal, the preservation and protection of more wildlife habitats, the introduction of new environmental practices, and the incorporation of aboriginal people into forest management.

Three interpretive forests along Highway 99 are open to the public. The Brohm Lake Interpretive Forest, near popular Brohm Lake, is located north of the Alice Lake Provincial Park turnoff. For more information on the Whistler Interpretive Forest, see page 129. Eighteen kilometres north of Whistler, Shadow

Lake Interpretive Forest is a 125-hectare park with trails for walking, hiking, biking, snowshoeing, and cross-country skiing. Shadow Lake is aptly named, hidden behind a wall of second-growth forest. Loop trails between the highway and the Soo River lead through areas of managed and natural forest. The short loop trail can be hiked in under 10 minutes.

Road to D'Arcy

The Pemberton Portage Road to D'Arcy, known locally as Portage Road, is only 38 kilometres long. On the surface, the trip is uneventful. A little exploration into the area reveals an enormous recreation potential.

In addition to Birkenhead Lake Provincial Park, there are four recreation sites, two recreation trails, a rustic resort, and a private campsite with boat access. The Anderson Lake Band (452-3221), which makes up the largely Native community of D'Arcy (population 60), also operates the Gates Creek salmon project. Community powwows and gatherings are occasionally held; the public is welcome to attend.

Once the overland portage from Lillooet to Anderson lakes, the road was recently paved. Some sections are straight and easy, running beside local farmlands where cattle and log barns predominate. Other sections require patience as the road narrows. There is occasionally limited visibility. Overall, however, the route is fairly easy. The

Recreation highlights along Portage Road

Ivey Lake
A 9-hectare lake with a catch-and-release fishery for large rainbow trout, up to 3 kilograms. A gravel BC Hydro access road leads to the lake, 4 kilometres north of Mount Currie.

Mosquito Lake
Beach, fishing, swimming, picnicking. A small, forested site immediately to the east of Ivey Lake. Receives low use. Access road is two-wheel-drive but may be muddy and rutted in wet weather. Caution: wharf and footpath at lake may be slippery.

Owl Creek
Camping, motorhomes, fishing, picnicking. A large, semi-open area divided into two sites, one on Owl Creek and the other on the Birkenhead River. Access by gravel road, suitable for all vehicles. This site receives low use.

Owl Lake Trail
From Owl Creek, the round trip is 7 kilometres, elevation gain 140 metres. The trail follows through a forested valley bottom. Trailhead is accessible by four-wheel-drive vehicle. Not recommended in wet weather.

Mount Ronayne Trail
Round-trip distance between Owl Lake Trailhead and Ogre Lake is 34 kilometres, elevation gain 750 metres. Trailhead is accessible by four-wheel-drive. Recommended for fit and experienced backpackers only. Trail extends beyond forested Owl Lake Chain and then ascends to the alpine backcountry enroute to Ogre Lake. The alpine section of the trail is a cairned route only.

Spetch Creek
Camping, fishing. A small, forested site that receives low use. Access by gravel road, not suitable for motorhomes.

Blackwater Lake
Camping, motorhomes, fishing, ice fishing, picnicking, nature tours. A small site on the road to Birkenhead Lake. Access by good gravel road but motorhomes not recommended because of site limitations. Receives low use.

Birkenhead Lake Provincial Park
Ninety-one campsites. Picnic area. Wood supplied, toilets, tables, litter barrels, boat launch, drinking water, day parking, sandy beach, swimming. Safe for children. Rainbow trout, Dolly Varden, kokanee. Excellent fishing in the 6-kilometre-long Birkenhead Lake. Within the park, forests are home to moose, deer, black bears, martens, bobcats, and river otters. Phelix Creek is a good area to view great blue herons stalking underwater prey.

Birkenhead River
Named for a British troopship sunk off the coast of South Africa in 1852. Fishing for chinook and coho salmon, Dolly Varden, steelhead and rainbow trout.

Birken
Located on Gates Lake, Birken is at the summit of the Cascade Mountains near Birken Pass, the highest point on the Douglas Trail. Birkenhead Resorts (452-3255) can be reached by car, or ask BC Rail to drop you enroute. Established in 1935, the resort includes a restaurant, a small store, and cabins. Rowboats and pedal boats can be rented. Fishing licences and tackle are sold. Gas is available.

Anderson Lake
Small resort community set beside lake. Water sports, grocery store, fishing supplies, cottages, gas, boat launch. Overnight camping is available at the Anderson Lake Resort and Gas Station (452-3232) and the Red Barn Campground (452-3406). Both are located at the end of the Pemberton Portage Road.

Llamas make unusual roadside friends

Portage Road is as close as you'll get to a gentle journey back in time.

Away to the gold fields

On Sunday, April 12, 1858, the wooden side-wheel steamer *Commodore* arrived in sleepy Victoria from San Francisco, loaded with 455 men. Thousands more would arrive within the next few months. In June, 7149 gold-seekers came from San Francisco alone.

The Cariboo gold rush had begun. As miners swarmed across the rugged landscape heading to the bars of the Fraser River, local resources were pushed to the limit. Halfway to the Cariboo gold fields, the town of Lillooet bulged with as many as 15,000 residents. Food was expensive,

travel dangerous, and accommodation scarce.

The Bridge River Valley, leading to today's communities of Seton Portage, Shalalth, Gold Bridge, and Bralorne, was first explored in 1858. Entering the Fraser River just north of Lillooet, the Bridge River was the site of a shantytown called Bridgeport. Miners crossed the Fraser River on a toll bridge. On weekends, Bridgeport filled with men relaxing, drinking, and swapping stories.

The discovery of gold affected other areas of the Bridge River Valley. Shalalth, located on Seton Lake, was the bottleneck for many heading inland in search of the mother lode. Later, a narrow, difficult trail was carved out over Mission Mountain into the gold

fields of the upper Bridge River Valley.

By the mid-1860s, the gold rush had moved north to Barkerville. The Bridge River Valley slipped once again into anonymity.

As you drive along Highway 40 from Lillooet to Gold Bridge, you'll pass placer mineral leases marked by wooden posts or stone cairns. Some of these claims are still worked today.

Placer claims are located beside creeks and rivers. Miners separate gold from gravel using a gold pan or sift it in a sluice box.

For more information about Lillooet and the area, see Altitude SuperGuide's *British Columbia Interior* guidebook.

Mining makes a town

In 1900, 20-year-old Delina C. Noel moved to the Bridge River Valley with her new husband, Arthur Noel. Mining folk, they followed on the heels of a gold strike in 1897 that revived interest in the area. Arthur bought a 50 percent interest in the Pioneer Mine, 3 kilometres up Cadwallader Creek near present-day Bralorne, the site of an 1865 strike. After two years of making $10 a day, Noel dropped out, leaving his partner to slog on alone. The Noels decided to work their own claims.

Their cabin, built at No. 2 Lorne Camp, was famous throughout the valley. A fireplace constructed with rock samples featured gold ore as highlights. On the wall, the hide of a huge grizzly shot by a 22-year-old Mrs. Noel was displayed.

At the age of 78, Mrs. Noel received a Dogwood Medallion from the BC government. The province's highest honour, it recognized her 58 pioneering years in the mining industry. Age didn't slow her down. She was still actively working her claim on Piebiter Creek in her mid-seventies.

By 1928, after changing hands several times, the Pioneer Gold Mine was again in production. Bralorne Gold Mines Ltd., destined to be Canada's richest gold mine, opened the same year.

Raw frontier towns boomed in the Bridge River Valley when the price of gold rose in the early 1930s. Communities sprung up, complete with banks, schools, churches, and social clubs. The 1935 voters list shows Bralorne Mine, population 368; Gold Bridge, 321; Minto, 146; Pioneer Mine, 345; and Tyaughton, 15.

Gold was the lifeblood of the area for more than 75 years. Bralorne, 107 kilometres

Gold panner's paradise

You can still pan for gold in Bridge River Country

ACCORDING TO THE BC Ministry of Mines, the public may pan for gold on Placer Mineral Leases with the owner's permission. Private property must be respected. The Government Agent in Lillooet sells a small booklet, *George's Guide to Claim Staking in BC*. Drop by the office at 651 Main Street for a copy, or telephone 256-7548.

The Gold Bridge area is also a rockhound's paradise. The largest single jade boulder recorded in the *Guiness Book of World Records* was found in the Noel Valley, near Bralorne.

west of Lillooet on Highway 40, was the heart of mining activity. Underground tunnels 160 kilometres long ultimately produced nearly 82.2 million grams of gold. Pioneer Mine's total production was 36.9 million grams. In 1959, the mines merged, becoming Bralorne Gold Mines Limited.

Over the years, more than 10,000 men and women worked in the mines. On average, 12 gold bricks were poured each month and sent by mail to the Royal Canadian Mint in Ottawa. In 1971, when Bralorne Gold Mines closed, the total value of gold produced exceeded $135 million.

Gold Bridge was the antidote to Bralorne's company town mentality. Free of restraints, it became a thriving enterprise centre, supported by Bralorne miners. Gold Bridge remains an active community of some 70 people.

Amenities include a hotel, motel, restaurant, gas station, grocery store, and recreation outfitters.

After the Bralorne mine closed, the Whiting Brothers purchased the 566.6-hectare town site. Hoping to turn the community into a year-round resort, they spent two years renovating the properties. In 1978-79, because of the ideal climatic conditions in the old mine, people took up growing mushrooms underground. In the 1980s, Bralorne mine was reopened for a time. Far from a ghost town, Bralorne is home to some 100 people.

The Bridge River Valley is emerging as a centre for outdoor recreation. Nearby lakes, including Big Gun, Little Gun, Carpenter, and Tyaughton, as well as surrounding mountain ranges, provide opportunities for sport fishing, year-round backroads, ATV expeditions,

wilderness camping, and backpacking. Winter sports like ice fishing, heli-skiing, cross-country skiing, snowshoeing, and snowmobiling are popular. Plans are under way to upgrade historic trails, such as the MacGillivray Pass route to a BC Rail stop on Anderson Lake and the Chism Trail to Birkenhead Lake.

Local people work with the Ministry of Highways and BC Hydro, and in tourism and service industries. Former townsites, like Brexton, Bradian, and Pioneer, are ghost towns. Every five years, a "last reunion" is held. The next one is in 1998. In the meantime, the Bralorne Mining Museum and Infocentre keeps the memories alive.

Sure-footed mountain friends

The Chilcotin Mountain Cayuse horse is a semiwild yet

Four-wheel-drive adventures

TWO ALTERNATE ROUTES lead to Bridge River Country. The Hurley Forest Access Road, referred to as "the summer road" or simply the Hurley by locals, is a great escape with the feel of four-wheel-drive travel. Most vehicles can make the grade without too much trouble, although this is not a drive for the fainthearted. Local forest districts recommend four-wheel-drive, but tour buses are known to cross the 45-kilometre mountain route to Gold Bridge. At the end of May, the road is plowed and graded and remains in good condition until late October. Weather can be changeable, however, and chains are recommended for the approximately two-hour drive.

To get to the Hurley, drive along the Pemberton Meadows Road to the point where the pavement ends. Turn right at the Coast Mountain Outdoor School turnoff, crossing over the Lillooet River bridge. Just past the bridge, a fork in the road heads steeply uphill to the right. This is the start of the Hurley Road. For information on seasonal road conditions, call or write the Squamish Forest District, 42000 Loggers Lane, Squamish, BC V0N 3G0; telephone: 898-2100.

A trickier four-wheel-drive adventure is the Highline Road. Anyone who successfully makes the 29.9-kilometre crossing from D'Arcy to Seton Portage is dubbed a "Highline Hero" by the

locals. Maintained by the Seton Portage-Shalalth District Chamber of Commerce, the Highline is rough and narrow, definitely not recommended for camper vans or other bulky vehicles. This is true four-wheel-drive adventure, with the possibility of meeting logging trucks enroute. Like the Hurley, the Highline's superb views make the challenge worth it. For a free brochure with a map of the Highline Road and Bridge River Valley, write the Seton Portage-Shalalth District Chamber of Commerce, Seton Portage, BC V0N 3B0. For information about road conditions and closures, call the BC Ministry of Highways at 1-800-663-4997.

The ghost town of Bradian may yet see a revival

Bralorne's historic trails

- **Lakes Trail:** This 4.4-kilometre trail links Kingdom, Noel, and Lost lakes. Perfect for either hiking or skiing, this gentle trail skirts beneath Mt. Fergusson (2593 metres). Kingdom and Lost lakes include forestry campsites; all three lakes have picnic tables.
- **Whynot Trail:** A steep trail ascending Fergusson Creek to about 1615 metres, where it joins an old mining road. At the first footbridge across Fergusson Creek, loop back to the lakes. The hardy can continue on the old road that climbs steeply to 2500 metres. From here, access can be gained to Mt. Truax and other peaks in the Bendor Range.
- **Waterloo Trail:** Starting at kilometre 7 on the Kingdom Lake Forest Road, this trail serviced the old Waterloo mine just beneath Mt. Fergusson. A steep climb leads to the old mine site at about 2100 metres just above a knoll at treeline. Mountaineers can walk the ridge to the northwest and descend steeply and carefully to the Whynot Trail or climb Mt. Fergusson peak.
- **Limestone Kiln:** An old limestone kiln built into a cave in the 1930s is an easy 2.1-kilometres from the same trailhead as Waterloo.
- **Powerline Trail:** Ideal for mountain bikes or skiing, this gentle 7-kilometre old road winds through a beautiful treed area above the Bralorne townsites.
- **Holland Trail:** A 0.6-kilometre hike leads to the Holland mine site from the 9-kilometre point on the Kingdom Lake Road. Old tailings and the remains of buildings can be seen. Access to Nomad Lake is gained by following flags up the steep slope past the Holland mine. This can be time-consuming because there are several rock slides to cross.
- **Andrea's Bear Hollow Trail:** This gentle 1-kilometre trail was the original road to Pioneer Mine, located 1.6 kilometres up Cadwallader Creek. Historical remnants include a 75-centimetre wooden stave waterline, which ran to the power house in the Bralorne townsite.
- **Sunshine Trail:** This old trail starts at the top of the community ski hill and proceeds up to treeline. From there, access is to Sunshine Mountain and other peaks of the Cadwallader Range. Skiing is often excellent in the Sunshine Basin right into May.

For more information and a map of the trails, write to the Bridge River Valley Chamber of Commerce, Gold Bridge, General Delivery, Gold Bridge, BC V0K 1P0, telephone: 238-2221.

gentle creature, born and bred in the Cariboo-Chilcotin region. These horses still roam free, in herds as large as 300. Harsh winters, heavy snows, difficult mountain passes, wildlife—Cayuse are bred to handle anything.

A short horse with a long head, Cayuse grow thick winter coats in the fall. In the winter, they feed in swamp meadows where the snow bends the grass into mats between 10 and 15 centimetres thick. They paw the snow away to reach the grass. In the spring, they feed from swamps, with their heads sometimes up to their eyeballs in water.

Horses like the ones used by Chilcotin Holidays Guest Ranch face a long training cycle. Most begin their careers at the age of three as packhorses. "This is the most important

Burgers, served picnic-style on the streets of Gold Bridge

part of their training," says owner-operator Kevan Bracewell. "All riders have been on horses that cut corners close to trees. Once a horse has been broke for packing, it's trained to give clearance for the packs. Later on, this saves the rider's knees."

Kevan knows his horses. A third-generation guide-outfitter, he comes from a pioneer Cariboo-Chilcotin family. He and his business partner, Sylvia Waterer, run pack trips, a guide school, and big-game viewing, as well as guest ranch trips.

Between 7 and 10 years of age, the Cayuse are ridden

Louis Skutnik: Caretaker of a ghost town

BRADIAN'S ALTERNATING red and green rooftops create a festive air that belies their lonely fate. Once described as "one of the prettiest towns ever created," the townsite, located 3 kilometres (1.8 miles) past Bralorne, is now a ghost town. Almost a ghost town, that is. Three of the original 80 homes have been renovated, and the rest are up for sale.

If you're passing through, you may meet Louis Skutnik, caretaker of the ghost town of Bradian. His home is the one with the sign over the door that says Jade for Sale. A Yugoslavian by birth, Louis arrived in Bralorne in 1965. After three years with the mine, he struck out on his own as a placer miner. At one time, he worked

Louis Skutnik

nine claims. In the late 1960s, he began making jewellery with local jade. He still works two claims, spending his winters in Arizona and his summers in Bradian.

As one of the few remaining old-timers, Louis has heard the rumours come and go over the years. "There's always talk of some company reopening the mine," he says.

While waiting for the next boom, he continues to pan for gold, a pastime he heartily recommends. "It's simple and fun," Louis says. "All you need is a gold pan, a spade, and waterproof boots. There's gold still there, especially in the old areas like Cadwallader and Noel creeks and the Bridge River. Just don't expect another gold rush."

Gold pans and other equipment are sold at the Bralorne Pioneer Store, telephone 238-2323.

Cayuse are trained to cover any kind of ground the South Cariboo has to offer

only by guides. Between 10 and 14, they are rotated among guides and expert riders. Only after reaching the age of 20 are the horses ridden by novices or children.

Flatland horses do not have the stamina of Mountain Cayuse, notes Kevan, and are a risk to riders in the Chilcotin's variable topography. Surefooted Cayuse can average 7315 vertical metres in a 10-hour day, covering a distance of 30 to 50 kilometres. They work six months of every year, in the summer and fall, totalling an average of 4800 kilometres a season.

From November to May, Chilcotin Holidays' trail horses feed at the ranch, located centrally within a 3200-square-kilometre guide territory. From May to November, the Cayuse rotate between camps and the range, with access to the variety of ranges within the Chilcotin Mountains. "During trips that involve a lot of riding, these horses can go up, over and down an average of six mountains a day," says Kevan.

Modern-day gambler

A certain kind of person falls in love with the Bridge River Valley. From the early gold rush days to the present, they're often gamblers of one sort or another. Gus Abel, the creator of Tyax Mountain Lake Resort, is one such gambler.

Gus's dream, back in the late 1970s, was to open a wilderness resort. A German immigrant, he explored BC for several years looking for the right location. Pouring over a set of maps showing weather patterns, he made an interesting discovery. There was a rel-

atively dry "desert" on the other side of the mountains from Whistler.

"On the Whistler side of the mountains, there were cedars and hemlocks, trees I associated with a wet climate," Gus recalls. "On the other side of the pass, there were ponderosa pines and Douglas-fir, which indicated dry weather. I went to look for it by car. It was very dry, but it was not a desert."

Gus found a property for sale on Tyaughton Lake, translated as "lake of the jumping fish" from the local Native language. "The property didn't look very good at the time. It was a real jungle." He bought it anyway, expending all his capital in the process. A year later, in 1982, he found an investor with a matching vision.

Construction of the lodge began in May 1986 at 100 Mile

Yellow spruce logs went into building Tyax Mountain Lake Resort, the largest log building on the West Coast

House. When it was completed, the spruce log building—believed to be the largest of its type in the Northwest—was dismantled and trucked to the lake in nine semitrailers. Just before Christmas, 1986, Tyax's doors opened for the first time. The luxury lodge is now completely self-contained, with a restaurant and lounge, 28 rooms, and a number of chalets for family rentals. Every form of skiing, fishing, hiking, and horseback riding is available. Gus Abel's gamble in the South Chilcotin has paid off.

Bridge River Valley amenities

Transportation
- Gold Bridge Airport: 238-2294

Recreation
- BC Hydro/Bridge River Community Recreation Site, Bridge River Power House: 259-8221
- Chilcotin Holidays Guest Ranch: 238-2274
- Spruce Lake Tours: 238-2425
- Tyax Mountain Lake Resort: 238-2221
- Tycat Ventures Snowcat Tours & Backcountry Skiing: 238-2221
- Valley Hardware: 238-2252 (fishing licences)
- Menhinick's Horse Rentals: 238-2375

Accommodations/Food
- Bralorne Inn Restaurant: 238-2525
- Chilcotin Holidays: 238-2274
- Gold Bridge Hotel & Restaurant: 238-2343
- Gold Dust Motel, Gold Bridge: 238-2423
- Lakeside Cottages, Shalalth: 259-8265

- Rippling Waters Campsite, Seton Portage: 259-8284
- Seton Portage Motel: 259-8355
- Sheri's Grill, Gold Bridge: 238-2596
- Tyax Lake Rentals: 238-2596
- Tyax Mountain Lake Resort: 238-2221

Groceries and gas
- Bralorne Pioneer Store: 238-2323
- Gallant's Junction General Store & Licensed Café, Seton Portage: 259-8342
- Gold Bridge Esso: 238-2456
- Gold Bridge Store: 238-2252
- Highline Pub, Seton Portage: 259-8207
- Seton Gas & Tire, Seton Portage: 259-8248

Other
- Bralorne Mining Museum and Infocentre: 239-2340. Open seasonally.
- Bridge River Valley Chamber of Commerce, Gold Bridge: 238-2221

- Lillooet Chamber of Commerce: 256-7262
- Lillooet Museum and Infocentre: 256-4308
- *Lillooet News:* 256-4210
- Seton Portage-Shahalth District Chamber of Commerce: 259-8342
- Seton Portage-Shalalth Travel Infocentre: 259-8383. Open seasonally.

Special Days
February
- Bradian Daze (Winter sports and snowmobile events)

May
- Spring Scoot (motorcross racing event), Victoria Day weekend, Seton Portage

June
- Only in Lillooet Days

July
- Canada Day Celebrations
- Bralorne Ball Tournament

August
- Gold Bridge Daze/BC Day Celebrations

References

Information
Calling Sea to Sky Country,
including Vancouver, use area code 604.

If you are dialing long distance within the province, dial 1, then 604, followed by the seven-digit number listed in this guide. If you have problems getting through, check with the operator. Telephone numbers listed throughout the book are subject to change without notice.

Tourist Information
- Tourism Association of Southwestern British Columbia, 204-1755 West Broadway, Vancouver, BC V6J 4S5, 739-9011; Canada/US toll-free: 1-800-667-3306. *The Vancouver and Southwestern British Columbia Travel Planner*, updated annually, is available free of charge from the association.
- Tourism Vancouver, Plaza Level, Waterfront Centre, 200 Burrard Street, Vancouver, BC V6C 3L6. Information line: 683-2000, Reservation line: 683-2772. Tourism Vancouver offers a wide range of brochures and information on activities in the Lower Mainland and other BC destinations.
- Discover British Columbia (not a walk-in office). Travel information and accommodation: 663-6000, Canada/US toll-free: 1-800-663-6000. Ask for Discover BC's annual, free of charge *British Columbia Accommodations* and its outdoor and adventure guides.

Travel Infocentres
British Columbia has more than 140 Travel Infocentres throughout the province. Of these, more than 75 are open year-round.

Free maps, brochures, and advice from local residents are provided at the following Travel Infocentres along Highway 99.
- Lillooet Travel Infocentre (seasonal), 790 Main Street, Box 441, Lillooet, BC V0K 1V0, 256-4308
- Pemberton Travel Infocentre. Open May–September. Located at the junction of Highway 99 and Portage Road. Box 370, Pemberton, BC V0N 2L0, 894-6175
- Seton Portage Travel Infocentre (seasonal). Seton Portage Road, Box 2066, Seton Portage, BC V0N 3B0, 259-8383
- Squamish Infocentre. Open year-round. Downtown Squamish at 37950 Cleveland Avenue beside the Squamish Pavilion, 892-9244. Note: The Squamish Infocentre, Business Information Centre, and Squamish and Howe Sound District Chamber of Commerce are all in the same building.
- Vancouver Travel Infocentre, 200 Burrard Street, Vancouver, (walk-in office), 683-2000
- Whistler Infocentre & Whistler Chamber of Commerce. Open year-round. Located at the junction of Highway 99 and Lake Placid Road (the first set of lights heading north on Highway 99 into Whistler), 932-5528
- Whistler Village Satellite Infocentre Booths. Open mid-June to Labour Day weekend, located in Whistler Village. One booth is located in Village Square and another at the bus loop on the right-hand side of the road off Village Gate Boulevard.

Squamish
- Sea to Sky Activity Centre, Box 1379, Squamish, BC V0N 3G0. Located under the blue roof at 38412 Cleveland Avenue in Squamish. 892-1025. Handles bookings for cruise packages, mountain bike and kayak tours, llama hikes, accommodations, and other recreation activities in the Squamish area.

Whistler Resort
- Whistler Activity and Information Centre. The Whistler Activity and Information Centre makes it easy to plan both group tours and individual activities. Stop in the office located at the front doors of the Whistler Conference Centre, or call 932-2394.
- Whistler Central Reservations 932-4222. Toll-free from Vancouver: 664-5625. BC/Canada/US toll-free: 1-800-944-7853; Fax: 932-7231
- Whistler Resort Association Administration Offices, 4010 Whistler Way, Whistler BC V0N 1B4, 932-3928, Fax: 932-7231
- Whistler Mountain Ski Corporation. Guest Relations, PO Box 67, Whistler BC V0N 1B0, Toll-free from Vancouver: 664-5614. BC/Canada/ US: 932-3434; Fax: 938-9174
- Blackcomb Mountain Guest Relations 687-4712. From Vancouver: 687-1032 (to switchboard). BC/Canada/US: 932-3141
- Blackcomb Hotel and Resorts. Reservations: 4557 Blackcomb Way, Whistler, BC V0N 1B4, 932-2882. BC/Canada/US toll-free: 1-800-777-0185; Fax: 932-2176
- Blackcomb Skiing Enterprises Ltd. 4545 Blackcomb Way, Whistler, BC V0N 1B4. Toll-free from Vancouver: 687-1032. BC/Canada/US: 932-3141; Fax: 938-7527

Other important numbers
Reporting Forest Fires
Dial 0 and ask for Zenith 5555. Please report all forest fires immediately.

Hunting and Fishing
For information about hunting and freshwater fishing, consult the BC Fishing and Hunting Regulations or contact the Fish and Wildlife Conservation Officer in Squamish at 892-5971. The Sport Fishing Information Line is 1-800-663-9333.

Information on fishing in tidal waters is available from the Fishery Officer in the Department of Fisheries and Oceans in Squamish at 892-3230.

Provincial Parks

Direct specific questions about parks to Provincial Parks, Garibaldi District Office (898-3678), or the North Vancouver Office (929-1291).

RCMP (Royal Canadian Mounted Police)

Emergency: 911
Non-emergency: Squamish: 898-9611, Whistler: 932-3044, Pemberton: 894-6126

Timetables

BC Ferries 24-hour information line: 277-0277, BC Rail: 631-3500, BC Transit: 261-5100

24-hour road reports

525-4997: Lower Mainland.
938-4997: Whistler

Driving in British Columbia

Operating a motor vehicle while impaired is an offence under the Criminal Code of Canada. The maximum speed limit on the Sea to Sky Highway is 80 km/h (50 miles per hour). The use of safety belts and child restraints is required by law in British Columbia. Highway 99 is subject to temporary road closures. Helmets are required for motorcyclists in BC.

Ministry of Highways Road Information

Vancouver: 525-4997, Greater Victoria: 387-4997, Whistler: 938-4997. All other areas of BC, toll-free: 1-800-663-4997

BCAA Emergency Road Service

From Vancouver and the Lower Mainland: 293-2222. From outside the Lower Mainland, toll-free: 1-800-663-2222. BCAA Head Office: 268-5000.

BC Visitor Information

Visitors should obtain health insurance before coming to BC.

Any other health insurance plan may only provide partial coverage for services rendered outside the borders of your country of residence. Revolvers, pistols, and fully automatic firearms are prohibited entry into Canada.

Television road reports

Rogers Cable Television broadcasts road reports on the Information Network Channel three times an hour daily. The Weather Network Channel broadcasts road conditions every hour (November-April).

Radio road reports

Frequent road reports are broadcast on Mountain FM Radio: Squamish area: 107.1 FM, Whistler area: 102.1 FM, Pemberton area: 104.5 FM

Recommended Reading

Adams, Paul. *Whistler and Region Outdoors.* Vancouver, BC: Tricouni Press, 1993.

Basque, Garnet. *Fraser Canyon and Bridge River Valley.* Langley, BC: Sunfire Publications Limited, 1985.

Bostwick, Mark. *The Four-Wheeler's Companion.* Madeira Park, BC: Harbour Publishing, 1991.

Christie, Jack. *Day Trips from Vancouver.* Vancouver, BC: Greystone Books, 1989.

Christie, Jack. *The Whistler Outdoors Guide.* Vancouver, BC: Greystone Books, 1992.

Clemson, Donovan. *Backroad Adventures through Interior British Columbia.* Surrey, BC: Hancock House, 1981.

Colebrook, Bob; Kevin Raffler; and Jennifer Wilson. *The Whistler Handbook.* Whistler, BC: B+B Design and Publications, 1993.

Coward, Garth. *Tree Book: Learning to Recognize Trees of British Columbia.* Victoria, BC: Forest Service Information Division and Forestry Canada, 1992.

de Hullu, Emma, in collaboration with Evelyn E. Cunningham. *Bridge River Gold.* 2nd ed. Bridge River Valley, BC, 1993.

Domico, Terry. *Wild Harvest: Edible Plants of the Pacific Northwest.* Surrey, BC: Hancock House, 1979.

Doughty, Heather. *Ski British Columbia.* Edmonton, BC: Lone Pine Publishing, 1991.

Duff, Wilson. *The Indian History of British Columbia,* vol. 1. Victoria, BC: British Columbia Provincial Museum, 1965.

Edwards, Irene. *Short Portage to Lillooet.* Mission, BC: Cold Spring Books, 1985.

Hobson, Clive. *The Insider's Guide to the Best Canadian Skiing.* New York, NY: Fodor's Travel Publications, 1992.

Macaree, Mary and David. *103 Hikes in Southwestern British Columbia.* 3rd ed. Vancouver, BC: Douglas & McIntyre, 1987.

McGill, Bryan, editor-in-chief; Cheryl Coull, and Anne Mayhew executive editors. *Beautiful British Columbia Travel Guide.* Victoria, BC: Beautiful British Columbia, 1994.

McLane, Kevin. *Squamish The Shining Valley,* Squamish, BC, Merlin Productions, 1994.

Patterson, Bruce, and Mary McGuire. *The Wild West.* Banff, AB: Altitude Publishing, 1993.

Peterson, Roger Tory. *A Field Guide to Western Birds.* Boston, MA: Houghton Mifflin Company, 1990.

Pratt-Johnson, Betty. *141 Dives in the Protected Waters of Washington and British Columbia.* West Vancouver, BC: Gordon Soules Book Publishers, 1992.

Roberge, Claude. *Hiking Garibaldi Park at Whistler's Back Door.* Vancouver, BC: Douglas & McIntyre, 1982

Underhill, G. E. (Ted). *Alpine Wildflowers.* Surrey, BC: Hancock House, 1986.

Underhill, G. E. (Ted). *Upland Field and Forest Wildflowers.* Surrey, BC: Hancock House, 1986.

Van Tighem, Kevin. *Wild Animals of Western Canada.* Banff, AB: Altitude Publishing, 1992.

White, Gordon R. *Stein Valley Wilderness Guidebook.* Vancouver, BC: Stein Wilderness Alliance, 1991.

Woodward, Meredith Bain, and Ron Woodward. *British Columbia Interior.* Banff: Altitude Publishing, 1993

Index

Index

Photographic Credits

The BC Museum of Mining: 26, 27
Barry Bateman: 125
Brew Creek Lodge: 122
Constance Brissenden: 11, 18, 21, 22, 36, 40a, 61, 138, 139, 141, 142a&b, 144a, 145, 146b, 151, 152a&b
Chateau Whistler Resort: 54, 55a, 62
Chilcotin Holiday Guest Ranch: 153
C.P. Czartoryski: 25, 109, 144b
Al Harvey: 6, 8, 10, 30, 31a-c, 50a, 50c, 51a, 58, 67, 68, 72, 74, 75a&b, 84, 86b, 91, 99, 123, 129, 131, 149.
Joseph King: 17
Douglas Leighton: 12, 14, 15, 146a
Randy Lincks: front cover, 44-45, 64, 66b, 73, 127, 130, back cover
Larry Loyie: 160
Isobel MacLaurin: 119
Bonny Makorewicz: front cover left inset, 19, 76-77, 76, 77b&c, 78, 81, 82, 85, 88, 92, 93b, 94, 95, 120, 135
Paul Morrison: 55b, 79
Owl Creek Llama Treks: 148
Photo Hunters Freelance: 32, 35, 37, 93a
Maureen Provencal: 80
Alec Pytlowany: 51b
Leanna Rathkelly: front cover right inset, 28, 48, 83, 104, 111, 114, 115, 117a, 128
Dennis Schmidt: 41, 43, 103a&b, 117b
Esther Schmidt: 7, 102, 103c, 136
Sewell's Marina: 20
Squamish Library: 13
Squamish Reserve: 34b
David Stoecklein: 126
Peter Timmerman: 2, 24, 40b, 42, 50b, 96, 116, 132, 134
Tyax Mountain Lake Resort: 154
Vancouver Public Library: 34a, 46
Brent Wallace: 112-113
Whistler Mountain Resort Association: 89, 66a, 90, 97, 98, 106-7, 110, 118a, 118b, 124
Whistler Museum: 47, 87

Acknowledgements

Additional research and editorial assistance: Warren J. Pawluk. Thanks to the following for their help and advice: to friends and writing associates Larry Loyie, Glen Helmlinger, Ron Woodward, Meredith Bain Woodward, Karen Essex, Callan Tay, Shea Montgomery, Gail Buente, Alma Lee, Oxana Macura, Deanna Pilling, Kathy Wallace, Shawn and Stan Wallace, Fraser Andrew, Lori Ternes and to the West Vancouver Permits and Licences, Al Midnight (BC Parks), Tom Bell (BC Parks), Ministry of Forests, Jim Hegan (Ministry of Transportation and Highways), BC Association of Forest Companies, John Tisdale (Squamish Forest Service), Billy Hoskin (Squamish Forest Service), Vancouver Public Library, Squamish Public Library, Whistler Museum and Archives, BC Museum of Mining, Squamish Chamber of Commerce, District of Squamish, BC Ministry of Tourism, Harbour Ferries Ltd., Tom Sewell (Sewell's Marina), Tourism Association of Southwestern BC, Squamish and Howe Sound Chamber of Commerce, Mayor Ted Nebbeling, Resort Municipality of Whistler, BC Wildlife Branch, Ministry of Land, Environment and Parks, Squamish Nation (Squamish), Mount Currie Band (Mount Currie), Anderson Lake Band (D'Arcy), Nancy Greene-Raine, Steve Podborsky, Whistler Mountain Ski Corporation, Blackcomb Skiing Enterprises Limited Partnership, Chateau Whistler, Whistler Centre for Business and the Arts, Whistler Resort Association, Jane Cyr (BC Rail Corporation), Pat Stephens (BC Ferries), Graham Underhill (Bowen Island Realty), Staples & Company, Doug Banner (Alpine Adventure Tours), Kevin McLane, Shelly Mallin, Dona Sturmanis, and many, many others.

About the author

Constance Brissenden

Constance has written about British Columbia for more than a decade. Her first assignment was a series on its rivers for *The Province Weekend Magazine*, which took her rafting, floating and fishing her way across the province.

She has authored five non-fiction books, written more than 1800 articles for magazines and newspapers, and interviewed and profiled hundreds of subjects. Her articles have appeared in *The Globe & Mail, Maclean's, Toronto Calendar Magazine, City & Country Home, Western Living, BC Business, V Magazine, BC Woman, Chinese Edition* and many others.

As head writer and managing editor of EXPO '86, Constance supervised hundreds of feature stories, four versions of the *Expo 86 Guidebook* and the Exposition's final report. She is the author/editor of *Info to Go: For Women on the Go* and *Triple-O: The White Spot Story.* She is currently working on a new project, *Living Traditions of the First Nations*, with Cree co-writer Larry Loyie.

Constance loves to travel, and continues to enjoy the many adventures and pleasures of Whistler and Sea to Sky Country.